COLLINS

garden
wildlife

D1470926

COLLINS

RSPCA GUIDE TO

garden wildlife

ATTRACTING WILDLIFE TO YOUR GARDEN

VAL PORTER

ILLUSTRATIONS BY JUSTINE PEEK

HarperCollins*Publishers*

First published in hardback in 1996 by
HarperCollins*Publishers*
77-85 Fulham Palace Road
Hammersmith, London W6 8JB

The HarperCollins website address is:
www.**fire**and**water**.com

This edition first published in paperback in 1999

00 02 03 01 99
2 4 6 8 7 5 3 1

A catalogue record for this book is available from the British Library

This book was created by
The Templar Company plc, Pippbrook Mill, London Road, Dorking, Surrey RH4 1JE
Designed by Caroline Reeves
Edited by Robert Snedden

ISBN 0 00 413383 8

Set in Garamond
Colour origination in Singapore, by Colourscan
Printed and bound by Printing Express Ltd., Hong Kong

Photographic Credits

p. 2 FLPA/David Hosking; p. 6 Mark Hamblin; pp. 8/9 FLPA/Rolf Bender; p.10 Mark Hamblin; p.11 FLPA/N. Clark; p.12 RSPCA/Tim Thomas; p.13 FLPA/David Hosking; p.14 RSPCA/Colin Seddon; p.17 FLPA/Eric and David Hosking; pp. 20/21 RSPCA/Stuart Harrop; p. 25 top RSPCA/Duncan McEwan, centre and bottom RSPCA/E.A. Janes; p.28 FLPA/B. Borrell; p.31 RSPCA/Stuart Harrop; p.32 RSPCA/Stuart Harrop; p.34 RSPCA/Mr and Mrs R. P. Lawrence; p.37 (both) RSPCA/Jonathan Plant; p.38 top RSPCA/Duncan McEwan, bottom RSPCA/Jonathan Plant; p.39 top left RSPCA/Jonathan Plant, top right RSPCA/Ross Hoddinott, bottom left RSPCA/E.A. Janes, bottom right RSPCA/Jonathan Plant; p.41 RSPCA/Peter Stiles; p.43 top FLPA/H. Clark, centre FLPA/Mike Rose, bottom FLPA/P. Heard; p.44 RSPCA; p.45 RSPCA/David Stiles; p.46 FLPA/B.B. Casals; p.48 (both) FLPA/G.E. Hyde; p. 50 left FLPA/G.E. Hyde, right RSPCA/Dr W.J. Wall; p. 51 FLPA/B. Borrell; p.52 RSPCA/Duncan McEwan; p.53 FLPA/W. Rohdich; pp. 54/55 RSPCA/Stuart Harrop; p.56 FLPA/Eric and David Hosking; p.57 FLPA/Chris Mattison; p.61 left FLPA/D.T. Grewcock, right FLPA/W.J. Hawes; p.62 FLPA/Leo Batten; p.63 FLPA/R. Bender; pp. 64/65 FLPA/W. Rohdich; p.66 left RSPCA/Stuart Harrop, right RSPCA/Colin Carver; p.67 FLPA/R. Wilmshurst; p.74 FLPA/S.C. Brown; p.75 FLPA/W. Rohdich; p.76 RSPCA/E.A. Janes; p.77 RSPCA/Colin Carver; p.78 Mark Hamblin; p.83 FLPA/Roger Tidman; pp. 84/85 FLPA/Eric and David Hosking; p.86 RSPCA/E.A. Janes; p.88 RSPCA/Mr and Mrs R. P. Lawrence; p.89 RSPCA/E.A. Janes; p.92 RSPCA/E.A. Janes; p.93 RSPCA/Mr and Mrs R. P. Lawrence; p.98 RSPCA/E.A. Janes; p.100 RSPCA/Mavis Dean; p.101 FLPA/Eric and David Hosking; p.102 RSPCA/Colin Carver; p.104 RSPCA/John Howard; p.105 FLPA/John Hawkins; p.106 left RSPCA/E.A. Janes, right FLPA/E.E. Casals; p.107 RSPCA/Colin Carver; p.112 RSPCA/Mr and Mrs R. P. Lawrence; p.114 FLPA/R. Thomson; p.115 RSPCA/E.A. Janes; pp. 118/119 RSPCA/E.A. Janes; p.120 FLPA/M.B. Withers; p.121 RSPCA/Colin Seddon; p.123 RSPCA/Stuart Harrop; p.127 RSPCA/Colin Carver; p.132 RSPCA/Stuart Harrop; p.139 FLPA/T. Wharton; p.141 FLPA/Hugh Clark; p.145 RSPCA/Jonathan Plant; p.146 top RSPCA/Colin Carver, centre RSPCA/E.A. Janes, bottom FLPA/M.B. Withers; p.148 RSPCA/E.A. Janes; p. 149 (both) FLPA/R. Hosking; p.152 RSPCA/E.A. Janes; p.153 RSPCA/Colin Carver

Contents

Foreword

The Royal Society for the Prevention of Cruelty to Animals (the RSPCA) was founded in 1824 to promote kindness and to prevent cruelty to animals. It is the world's oldest and largest charity dedicated to animal welfare.

Few people realise that much of the Society's workload is taken up by the welfare of wild animals as well as that of the more familiar domestic and farmyard breeds. The RSPCA's team of 300 inspectors based throughout England and Wales is called upon to help thousands of wild animals in distress each year. These might range from swans caught in fishing tackle to badgers injured by wire snares or bats trapped in houses. They will also carry out investigations into possible infringements against wildlife legislation.

The RSPCA has three specialised wildlife hospitals available to care for wild animal casualties, with the aim of rehabilitating them back to the wild if at all possible. The expertise and experience gained by the RSPCA is freely shared with others involved in similar work.

However, it is most often day-to-day contact with animals in their 'backyard' that results in people contacting the Society. They want to know about such diverse matters as what to do with unwanted frogspawn and how to help abandoned fledglings, or perhaps they want to know more about the fox visiting their garden or the snake they've suddenly discovered in the pond. People also ask the RSPCA for advice on what to feed birds and the best places to site nesting-boxes.

It is for these reasons that the RSPCA welcomes the opportunity to co-operate in the production of this book. Encouraging an interested and caring attitude towards the wildlife on our doorsteps can only be of benefit to the animals. We hope it will also provide an insight into the natural world, and a great deal of pleasure, for the wildlife-friendly gardener.

Happy watching!

Colin Booty
Tim Thomas
RSPCA Wildlife Department

Wild Gardens

As a variety of habitats are eroded, invaded, polluted and disappear altogether, gardens become increasingly important refuges for wildlife. Every garden, no matter its size or location, from the grounds of grand country houses to the backyard urban patch, can be a wildlife haven, and every gardener can truly make a difference in wildlife's battle to survive in an increasingly hostile world.

One of the aims of this book is to describe the wild creatures that might live in or pass through your garden and to explain why they are there, what they are doing, and where and when to look for them. In addition, we hope to inspire you to encourage wildlife by understanding its needs and how best you can meet them. The book also gives an idea of the benefits that wildlife can bring – to you, to your garden and to the environment as a whole – including the great pleasure and interest of watching wildlife right on your own doorstep.

HABITATS AND NICHES

An organism's habitat is the place where it lives, its address in the natural world. Some organisms are adaptable and have more addresses, more places where they are at home, than others. Most gardens, on whatever scale, contain damp areas, sunny corners, rough patches, shrubbery and plants (including weeds), pockets of exposed soil, and places to hide under or behind – a variety of desirable residences for wildlife.

A song thrush comes to drink at a garden pond. Mature, suburban gardens are ideal for this bird.

An organism's niche describes the way it relates to and interacts with its environment, both the physical elements of that environment and the other organisms within it. Think of it as something akin to the organism's job description. In the garden there are a diversity of habitats and niches within a small space – a number of places to live and jobs to be filled.

The needs of each species are different and the greater the diversity of habitats in a garden, the greater the variety of wildlife that will make use of them. But it is important to look at each garden in the context of its surroundings when considering the living things that might make a home there.

NO GARDEN IS AN ISLAND

There is little point in creating a pond at the heart of a million square miles of desert and expecting an explosion of wildlife. If there are no corridors along which it might reach your oasis, the wildlife will not come. However marvellous the facilities at your plush new environmental address it will remain unoccupied if there is no way for life to get there. The 'desert' might be literally one of sand; but equally it could be city concrete or intensive agriculture or a conifer plantation.

Imagine yourself hovering high above your garden so that you can see the surrounding landscape. Then imagine yourself as an animal in that landscape.

Roe deer eating roses in a south London garden.

Your garden does not exist alone in space: it has a context, it has surroundings, which may or may not be hospitable to wildlife. The first species to colonise your garden will be those that already exist around it.

Islands can be sanctuaries but equally they can be prisons. Organisms also need the means of staying in touch with others of their kind, for mating and propagating the species, and for their offspring to be able to disperse and find new territories when local resources don't grow with the population.

GREEN CORRIDORS

It is noticeable in recent years how some wildlife species have become almost more common in urban areas than in the countryside. The twentieth century has seen their rural habitats greatly depleted, especially with the tremendous increase in intensive agriculture and forestry and the rapid spread of urbanisation.

Many animals have been fleeing towards the towns, where they can often find plenty of food and all sorts of unlikely homes. Often they have used the networks of vegetation along railway embankments and canals to reach these new habitats. Some species are now exploiting motorway verges (which have become veritable wildlife havens) to spread to new areas. Like humans on the ancient ridgeways, wildlife uses these artificial corridors to exploit new habitats, and that is why urban and city gardens can make such a difference.

IDEAL HABITATS

So what are they searching for, these creatures on the move? Their first priorities are the essentials of life: food, water and shelter. Secondly, they need to find mates, breed, and raise a new generation. Not only do they need their

It is not only trains that use railway tracks. Animals will also make use of the green verges to travel between towns.

own 'patch', therefore, but they also need to meet others of their kind in the breeding season.

Suburban areas can be very appealing in this respect. The gardens offer chains of miniature territories, between which the creatures can move as the need takes them. People sometimes think of garden wildlife as 'their' wildlife, whereas it is much more likely that the birds, hedgehogs, foxes and badgers are busily doing the rounds of the local gardens, making the most of what is on offer. You can't expect to own wildlife!

Of course, there is no ideal garden for all wildlife and one of the first lessons to learn is acceptance of the limitations of your own garden, especially as regards those factors that you simply cannot influence, such as altitude, climate and latitude. But there is still much you can do to make your garden safer and more attractive for wildlife, and the chapters that follow will tell you how.

THE WEB OF LIFE

Imagine a tidy little garden, full of flowers and colour, very pleasing to the eye. You love birds and you put up nesting-boxes. A pair of blue tits take up residence and hatch out a family. You watch the parents busily carrying in food for the little ones, until suddenly they are no longer visiting the nest. You peer into the box and find the whole brood lying dead in the nest. Why? Because

Tits are valuable allies in the garden, particularly at nesting time when the adults take huge numbers of insects to feed the young birds.

you had been spraying the aphids that were beginning to exploit your roses. The blue tits had been feeding their young with those aphids and since you had cut off part of their food supply the nestlings had starved.

There is a huge and complex web of interactions and interdependencies between living things and their environment. A human tweak in one part of the web can have sometimes unexpected consequences in another part. The most important lesson for gardeners to learn is the need for balance – a balance that leads to harmony with wildlife, the ability to live with and understand the living world.

HAZARDS IN THE GARDEN

Wildlife faces many hazards in the garden. Some are obvious and some less so.

Nylon netting, used to protect fruit and vegetable crops, can trap and maim or slowly kill inexperienced young birds, snakes, amphibians, hedgehogs and others. The material has no 'give', and if animals get caught up they may be strangled in the mesh or become so entangled that they die slowly from shock, starvation and dehydration. If you really must use nylon netting, make sure that the mesh size is at least 4cm (1½in) and that the netting is always kept stretched taut.

Tennis nets and other sports nets can be a hazard, particularly for hedgehogs as they sometimes bumble into them and either try to push through head first, and get caught, or roll themselves up in a tangle of net and spines. Put nets away or keep them well clear of the ground when they are not in use.

Bonfire heaps that have been accumulating for ages are often a place of refuge for hedgehogs, lizards, grass snakes, toads and many over-wintering insects (including valuable ladybirds). They will be roasted alive, especially sleepy hibernators, unless you always make a point of moving the heap to a new site when you are ready to light it. Take care not to plunge your garden fork into a dozy animal while doing so.

Hedgehogs can easily get tangled in carelessly discarded drinks holders.

The same care should be taken with compost heaps, a favourite place for hibernating and nesting reptiles.

Strimmers and mowers can be lethal to slow-moving animals – hedgehogs in long grass, which tend to curl up at a threat of danger, or toads that simply squat down and stand their ground rather than moving away. Be especially careful in grass that is not mown or trimmed regularly, and be very wary in early summer when countless tiny frogs and toads struggling through grass can be minced by machinery.

Rubbish often traps or injures wildlife. Small rodents, for example, find their way into discarded bottles lying in ditches and can't climb up the glassy insides to escape; animals push their snouts into old yoghurt pots and tin cans and get stuck or lacerated, or they find themselves with a necklace of plastic from those collars that hold four-packs of drinks tins together – a hazard also for waterfowl. Always cut these 'nooses' before discarding them, even when putting them into your rubbish bin.

Ponds, pools and pits can trap animals unless there is a means of escape, such as a ramp, steps or perhaps a piece of chicken-wire hung vertically to act as a swarming net. Although an animal might be a perfectly adequate swimmer, it will soon become exhausted if it cannot leave the water in a pond or swimming-pool, and it will die from starvation if it cannot clamber out of a pit such as an empty swimming-pool or an unprotected drain or other hole.

Toxic chemicals should be used with great caution in the garden. Many creatures, for example, feed on invertebrates, which means that they will also ingest any poisons you have been using to kill off 'pests'. The section on green pest control suggests other ways of tackling unwanted invertebrates. Also think hard about substances that might pollute your pond if they are washed in by the rain – creosote, or salt, for example, as well as more obvious toxins such as weed-killers.

Welcoming wildlife

The other chapters in this book look more closely at the habits and needs of different groups. Diversity is the key but there is also the great problem of human perception. Many people are highly selective about the wildlife species they welcome into their gardens. They like hedgehogs, perhaps, but they don't want rabbits eating the wallflowers. They love to see butterflies, but pull out the nettles that are essential in the lifecycles of several species of butterfly. They are edgy about spiders; they declare war on slugs and ants; they are scared of bats… Their gardens become battlefields rather than havens.

These prejudices are often understandable and may run deep. But we hope that this book will help to remove some of them and show you how to live with those species you find undesirable, or at least find ways to deter rather than destroy them.

You also have to accept the realities of nature. For example, if you attract flocks of birds to your bird-table, you inevitably attract the birds' predators as well. That's life. You might find it upsetting if a sparrowhawk makes a lightning raid on the bird-table and takes one of 'your' birds but, after all, to the hawk it is as if you were deliberately laying out food on the wing for it. It only kills in order to live and the raids will make hardly a dent in the number of birds at your table, so why not admire the predator's skill and enjoy the opportunity of studying these handsome, agile birds at close quarters?

PETS AND WILDLIFE

Not all predators are indigenous wild species like sparrowhawks. A recent 'what the cat brought in' study suggested that at least 30 per cent of sparrow fatalities in an English village were caused by cats. Although this sounds alarming, many bird populations are perfectly capable of sustaining such losses. Even birds that have been only slightly injured by a cat often die within 48 hours, either from shock or, it is thought, because cats' teeth and claws may harbour bacteria that cause septicaemia in wounded birds. Cats also catch small mammals, especially rodents, and some develop the habit of swiping

at bats as they fly out of their roosts. If you do have a cat it is as well to be aware of its natural predatory instincts before encouraging wildlife.

In general, dogs are much less of a problem to garden wildlife as they rarely hunt like cats. But they can and do disturb wildlife, simply by their presence as much as by barking and chasing and digging things up.

Foxes and dogs, being related species, may come into conflict if a fox intrudes on a dog's garden territory. Cats, on the other hand, often seem to reach mutual if wary understanding with local foxes. If it ever does come to a direct contest, it is very often the fox that beats a hasty retreat, not the cat. It is extremely rare for a fox to kill a cat, although a smaller pet (such as a rabbit or guinea pig) is vulnerable, especially if left out-of-doors at night in an insecure hutch. Foxes are adept at finding weak spots in cages and are quite capable of ripping out ordinary chicken-wire.

In some circumstances wildlife can present a threat to pets, as they may pass on disease or parasites, and very rarely a pet might suffer from an adder bite. Even a toad can make an over-inquisitive dog uncomfortable.

GARDENS FOR WILDLIFE

To attract wildlife to your garden, you must first of all think small: attract the invertebrates by providing a wide variety of food and shelter plants, including as

A garden encounter between a cat and a fox.

many native species (from trees to weeds) as possible.

Insects like warm, sheltered areas so begin by providing shelter-belts (hedges, bushes, walls, fences with climbing plants) or making wind-protected corners that catch the sun. Trees, preferably of indigenous species, are ideal habitats for many insects as well as birds, and an oak tree (if you have room for it!) is the most magnanimous host of all. Among fruit-bearing small trees, hawthorns are invaluable.

The goat willow is another welcome tree, supplying nectar for insects early in the year. Silver birch is a good and quick-growing insect-friendly tree. Many insects are attracted by nectar and,

among the native shrubs and climbers, ivy is essential and brambles and honeysuckle are very useful indeed. Also try hazel (the nuts will attract several species of mammals) and berry plants such as elder, guelder rose, blackthorn and dog rose.

Plant lots of old-fashioned cottage-garden annuals and make space for wild flowers. Ideally, have a small wildflower meadow in which the grass is left uncut until it has gone to seed: the grass alone will become well populated with insect larvae. Plant night-scented flowers to attract moths – sweet rocket, evening primrose, nicotiana, night-scented stock, heliotrope, bladder campion, soapwort, everlasting pea – and have lots of

scented herbs such as marjoram, borage, lemon balm, mint, sage, chives and fennel. Your garden will soon be alive with insects!

It is also important to have plenty of undisturbed places like log piles, bits of rotting wood, stones and rocks, rough grass and other overgrown areas, undisturbed leaf litter, compost heaps and so on. These will give insects and other invertebrates food and shelter and somewhere to breed. A garden pond is a bonus as many invertebrates spend some of their lives in water. If you have a good invertebrate population, you will attract the birds, reptiles, amphibians and mammals that feed on them. To increase the attraction for these larger species,

give them peace to get on with the business of living unmolested, in unmanaged parts of the garden.

The ideal wildlife garden probably belongs to a lazy gardener, especially one who does not use pesticides and who does not welcome cats. More constructively, you can also offer supplementary feeding in difficult seasons and create habitats tailored to different species, as described in other parts of the book. Then just sit back and enjoy the pleasure and privilege of sharing your garden with wildlife. The longer you sit still, the more you will see. Lazy gardeners, rejoice!

Invertebrates

Take a look one summer day to see just how many small creatures are flying round your flowerbeds and going about their business in the jungle of your lawn. Insects, crustaceans, spiders, worms, slugs and snails are all part of the huge, amorphous group of animals called the invertebrates. Pollinating flowers, breaking down decaying plant and animal matter and providing a food source for other animals, they are an essential element of the wildlife garden's ecology.

Butterflies and moths

Despite their sometimes destructive caterpillars, butterflies and moths are usually welcome visitors to any garden. But why are some gardens so much more successful at attracting them than others? Essentially these insects need:

- food for the adults (nectar);
- food for the caterpillars (leaves);
- shelter from bad weather;
- safe places for eggs and other stages in the life cycle;
- somewhere to hibernate safely (if they do not migrate).

You can plant and design your garden to accommodate these needs. Each species needs specific plants on which to lay their eggs so that the caterpillars, when they hatch, have the right food to eat. Adult butterflies and moths consume mainly nectar, but it is not their sole food: red admirals and others like rotting windfall fruit and sap, and some of the hairstreaks eat honeydew from aphids.

The best way to distinguish between a butterfly and a day-flying moth is to look at the antennae. Those of a butterfly are knobbed at the tip.

GARDEN ATTRACTIONS

Provide an undisturbed stack of wood for hibernating butterflies and moths (it will also be a winter haven for queen bumble-bees and ladybirds). Make a sheltered, sunny place, ideally with a basking wall against which butterflies can spread their wings to absorb the warmth. A protected south-facing bank of wild honeysuckle, bramble and nettles will be a great attraction to several of the more colourful butterflies and the dramatic hawkmoths.

IN PRAISE OF THE STINGING NETTLE

Always have a sheltered, sunny patch of stinging nettles in your wildlife garden. It will be visited by some of the most handsome butterflies at egg-laying time: red admiral, peacock, comma, small tortoiseshell. Nettles are also a food plant for many other insects, including hoverflies and several moth species, and their seeds are eagerly devoured by birds.

PLANTING FOR BUTTERFLIES AND MOTHS

Nectar-rich plants:

aubrieta

bird's-foot trefoil

brambles

buddleia

clover

crab apple

everlasting pea

forget-me-not

Helichrysum

honeysuckle

lavender

marguerite

marigold

marjoram

Michaelmas daisy

primrose

privet

ragwort

rosemary

Rudbeckia

scabious

Sedum spectabile

sweet william

thistle

tobacco plant

traveller's joy

valerian

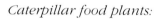

Caterpillar food plants:

bird's-foot trefoil

burdock

cabbage

charlock

clover

dog violet

hemp agrimony

holly

ivy

lady's smock

mignonette

nasturtium

stinging nettle

thistles

various grasses

marjoram (a), stinging nettle (b), traveller's joy (c),
clover (d), dog violet (e), bramble (f),
bird's-foot trefoil (g), thistle (h).

WHICH BUTTERFLY?

The most common garden butterflies are probably meadow brown, small tortoiseshell, large white, small white, green-veined white, brimstone, orange-tip, small skipper, peacock, comma and gatekeeper. In the south you might see white admiral, holly blue and various fritillaries. Immigrants that might visit summer gardens include clouded yellow, painted lady and red admiral.

Brimstone

Comma

Gatekeeper

Orange-tip

Small white

Green-veined white

Meadow brown

Large white

Small tortoiseshell

Small skipper

Peacock

Dark green fritillary.

White admiral

Holly blue

Painted lady

Clouded yellow

Common blue.

Red admiral.

WHICH MOTH?

Day-flying moths are often quite brightly coloured, like the red and black cinnabar moth (on ragwort), the red-spotted metallic burnets (which are poisonous to birds), and the black, white and orange magpie moth (which can devastate your currant bushes). There is one moth, the hornet moth, sometimes seen resting on a tree trunk by day, that looks very like a hornet; another, the humming-bird hawkmoth, flies very fast between its daylight hovers.

Most moths fly at night. Most of them are dull in colour, though several species surprise you by flashing their brightly coloured underwings. Other night-flying moths are dramatic more in size than in colour: there are some whoppers about! The convolvulus hawkmoth, for example, has a 12.5cm (5in) wingspan and a tongue 9cm (3½in) long.

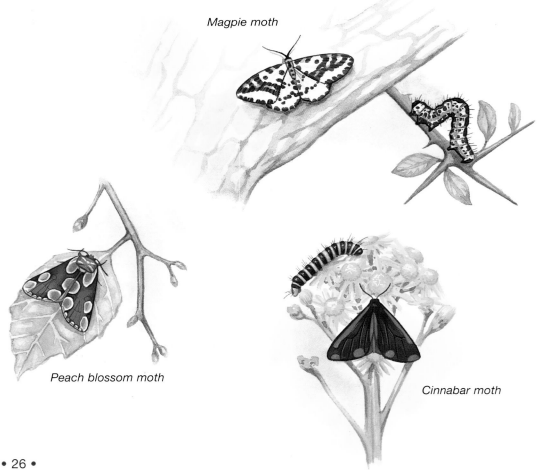

Magpie moth

Peach blossom moth

Cinnabar moth

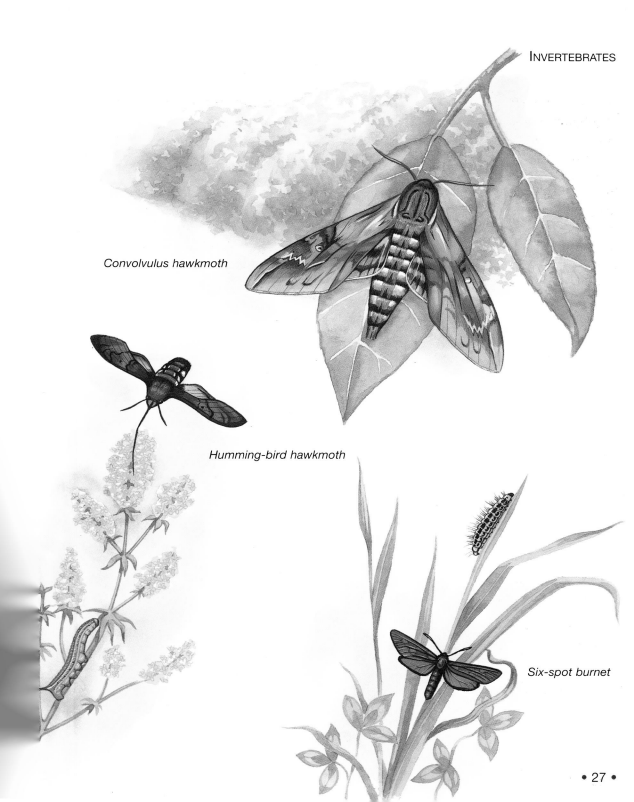

Convolvulus hawkmoth

Humming-bird hawkmoth

Six-spot burnet

LIFE CYCLES

The female butterfly or moth lays large numbers of eggs, either singly or in large clusters, on its host plant, the plant that its growing larvae will eat. A small tortoiseshell might lay up to a thousand eggs, for example, but many butterfly eggs are lost to predation or disease.

The larvae (caterpillars) emerge from the eggs, usually after 5 to 35 days, depending on the species. Some, for example the high brown fritillary, over-winter as eggs, hatching out in the spring.

The caterpillars grow rapidly as they consume the host plant. Most have to shed their skin several times as they grow.

The great majority of caterpillars succumb to predators or disease.

When fully grown the surviving larvae find a suitable hiding-place and each turns into a chrysalis (pupa). At this stage too, losses are high. You may find a chrysalis in leaf-litter or soil, wrapped in a small cocoon on a plant, hanging from a plant, or attached by a silken girdle to a plant stem.

The chrysalides eventually metamorphose into adult butterflies or moths. Most adults have a short life, lasting just long enough to mate and lay eggs, completing the insect's life cycle.

FINDING A CHRYSALIS

If you come across a chrysalis that seems to be vulnerable you could try to help, but you are unlikely to succeed. Keep the chrysalis damp by placing it on dampened moss, blotting paper, newspaper or potting compost, spraying the material with water whenever it begins to dry out. Have the chrysalis in a cage to protect it from predators, but do not bring it into a heated building: leave it somewhere in the shade outside or in a shed. Put twigs into the cage so that in due season the emerging butterfly or moth can climb on to them and spread its wings to dry. Release the butterfly

near its preferred host plants on a calm, sunny day, if possible when there are no birds waiting to snap it up. Moths should be released at night.

The pupa of a swallowtail butterfly is often suspended upright by silk threads.

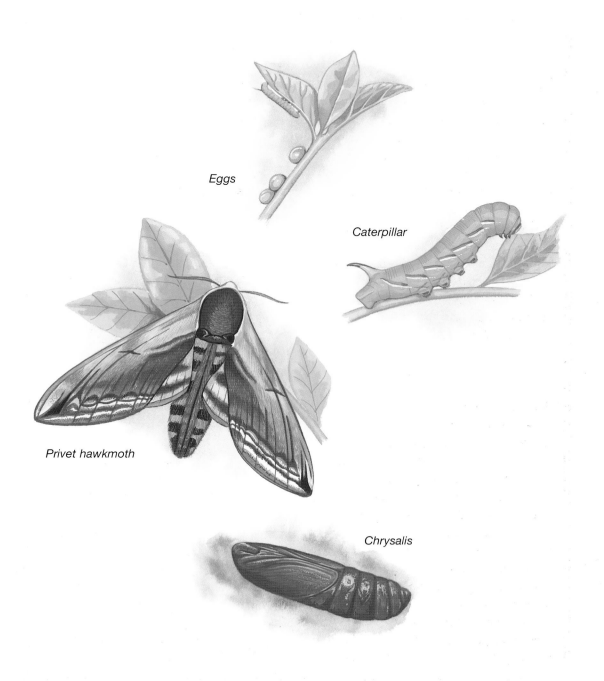

Eggs

Caterpillar

Privet hawkmoth

Chrysalis

HIBERNATION

Most species of butterfly and moth either migrate before winter or over-winter as chrysalides tucked away in garden sheds, log piles, behind bark, and so forth, or as eggs on the appropriate food plant. A few species over-winter as adults in tree-holes or will seek shelter in sheds, garages, greenhouses and homes.

Indoors they might choose somewhere unsuitable, such as behind a radiator or inside a fan heater or in the folds of curtains. You can try to persuade them to find a more suitable winter roost before they become really comatose or, if they are found later in the season, gently move them to a dark, undisturbed corner that does not get warm enough to waken them too early. Watch out for them as the weather warms up and make sure they can escape before they die of exhaustion flapping at a closed window.

PICKING UP A BUTTERFLY

Never handle a butterfly or moth by its wings. Pick it up very gently between thumb and forefinger on either side of the body.

CATERPILLARS

Be wary of touching a hairy caterpillar. The hairs might well cause skin irritation.

If you want to care for any caterpillar, you must identify the species so that you know its preferred food plant. Then put the caterpillar in a box with young leaves of that plant, cover the box to prevent escape and place it somewhere out of direct sunlight. Give it fresh leaves every other day and remove its droppings. Alternatively, put your caterpillar on a growing food plant and 'cage' it in a muslin sleeve; when it has eaten all the leaves in its cage, move it to another branch. If it is a moth caterpillar, it will probably get restless when it is ready to pupate, as it usually goes underground to do this.

HOME HIBERNATORS

Hibernation in the house is not confined to butterflies. You might find hibernating lacewings (often in large numbers in old cardboard boxes in a garden shed) and ladybirds. They often 'wake up' too early in the season because a room is warm and perhaps when the lights are on in the evening. If they are exhausting themselves batting against the lights, gently move them to a dark, cool place to continue their hibernation. You could offer them some home-made nectar or perhaps a small piece of soft fruit, like a pear – ladybirds particularly seem attracted to the moisture from this.

A peacock butterfly finds a place to hibernate among leaves in a garden shed.

ARTIFICIAL NECTAR FOR EARLY BUTTERFLIES

Dissolve a little honey in warm water; let it cool, soak a piece of cotton wool in the solution and put the cotton wool in a small dish for the insect to help itself. Or you can offer slightly diluted honey on the tip of a wooden ice-cream spatula or your finger.

Bees

All the numerous species of bee are vegetarian and the adult diet includes both nectar and pollen. Females often carry the pollen on their hairy legs or on their undersides, taking it back to the nest for their larvae. At the same time they also transport pollen from one flower to another, fertilising them so that seeds can be set.

Mining bees look rather like honey bees and often make their little mounded nests in lawns. Some species of bee will nest in existing holes in timber or masonry; others choose empty snail-shells, partitioning them with dung, or hollow tubes of straw, perhaps in a thatched roof.

HONEY BEES

Wild honey bees normally nest in hollow trees in colonies that might contain as many as 50,000 bees, all serving a single queen. There is no need to be alarmed if you see a swarm of honey bees: they have far better things to do than stinging you. The reason for swarming is usually that the queen is leaving with a mass of workers to seek new quarters after the hive has become overpopulated. They will settle somewhere, usually on a tree, sending out scouts to search for a new hive site. When a suitable site has been located the whole mass moves off to build a new nest.

There are at least a dozen species of bumble-bee, which are bigger and hairier than honey bees. They form colonies in underground nests – perhaps in a disused mousehole in a sunny bank, making a ball of grass and moss around the wax cells. Some species nest under stones whereas others prefer a higher nest: you might find them in an old bird's nest or in one of your bird nesting-boxes.

An early spring bee feeds on nectar and pollen.

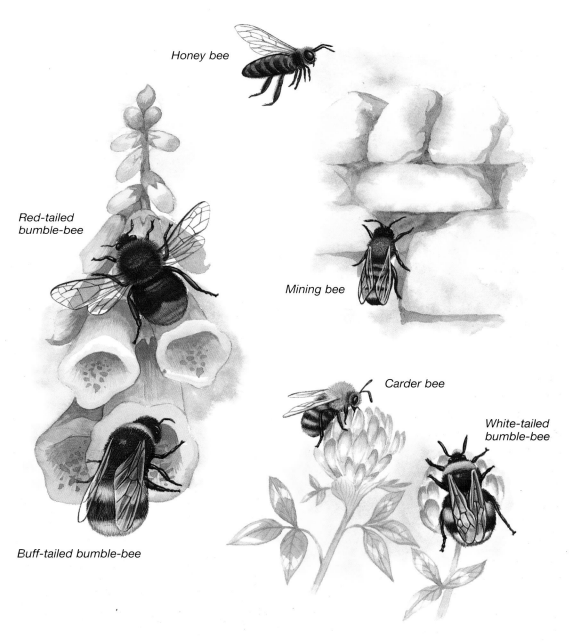

Honey bee

Red-tailed
bumble-bee

Mining bee

Carder bee

White-tailed
bumble-bee

Buff-tailed bumble-bee

All of the bees illustrated here are queens.

Wasps

Wasps are predators: they hunt for animal food for their larvae, though the adults often feed themselves on nectar and fruits. They use their stings for paralysing their insect prey as well as for self-defence.

Parasitic wasps include the metallic-coloured ruby-tailed or cuckoo wasps, the ant-like gall wasps, and chalcids and ichneumons. Digger wasps nest in woodworm holes, rotten wood, soil or sand and prey on a wide range of insects and small spiders. There are also some specialist spider-hunting wasps. Potter and mason wasps use clay and mud to make nests that are often vase-shaped or look like lumps of mortar.

Most wasp species are social rather than solitary. The familiar wasps that haunt your late summer picnic and orchard include the common wasp and the fairly similar German wasp, red wasp, tree wasp, Norwegian wasp and, biggest of all, the hornet. These social wasps all live in colonies, centred around a large queen. Their nests are built of wood pulp and you often see them rasping on wooden surfaces to collect nest-making material.

LIVING WITH WASPS

Unfortunately, wasps often choose to make their nests in places where you would rather they did not – in your loft, for example. This is only a real problem if people unwittingly put themselves between the nest entrance and the wasps that want to enter it. Get professional pest controllers to deal with such nests as soon as you notice the beginnings of nest-making.

Wasps will not sting you without reason, but they do sting in self-defence or to protect their nest. They can be of great help in the garden, preying on all sorts of other insects, so avoid the habit of automatically swatting them just because they are buzzing around you being a nuisance. Take an interest in them instead and you should soon lose your fear of them.

The nuisance period only lasts a short while from late summer to early autumn. As soon as the weather gets frosty they will disappear: only a few young queens will live through the winter, hibernating in log piles, outhouses, or in your home.

An extensive wasps' nest in a house attic.

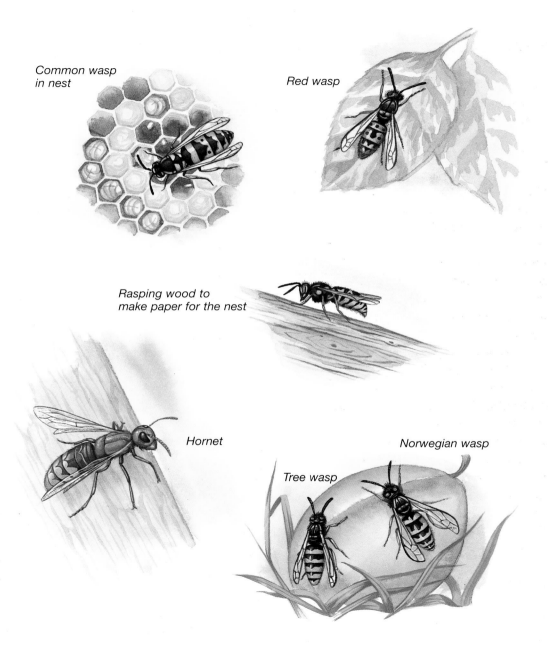

Common wasp
in nest

Red wasp

Rasping wood to
make paper for the nest

Hornet

Norwegian wasp

Tree wasp

Ants

Ants live in underground colonies centred on queens. Foraging workers set out in all directions from the colony in search of food.

The most common ants in the garden are the red ants (whose workers have quite vicious stings) and the black garden ants (with no sting) that you find under paving stones and paths and which 'farm' aphids for their honeydew. These black ants and the yellow meadow ants are the major swarm-fliers but their workers do not have wings.

Mating takes place in summer and early autumn. Great clouds of flying ants are ushered from their underground nests in nuptial swarms. In a striking, synchronised display, every colony in the area sends up its courting couples within moments of each other, filling the air with dancing ants. The clouds of insects make a great feast for birds, especially martins and swallows.

Black garden ants sometimes find their way into the house in search of sweet things to take back to the nest, but not very often. A more recent intruder which has taken up residence in some heated buildings is the small Pharaoh ant from North Africa.

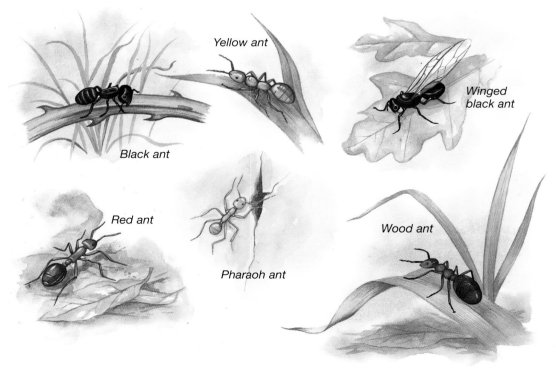

Yellow ant

Winged black ant

Black ant

Red ant

Pharaoh ant

Wood ant

Beetles

Beetles are among the most common types of animal on the planet. They can be found everywhere, from mountain tops to seashore, in marshes, woods, fields, ponds and streams and, of course, in your garden and in your home.

There are more different types of beetle than there are of any other kind of animal, with around 4000 varieties in Britain alone and more than a hundred times that number world-wide. Half of all the insects known are beetles.

A beetle's front pair of wings form a hard case that meets in a straight line down the animal's back. It is this feature more than any other that distinguishes the beetles from other insects. In most beetles the forewings almost completely cover and protect the hind body. Only the hindwings, which are folded neatly beneath the forewings when not in use, are used in flight. Some beetles fly reluctantly or have lost the ability to fly altogether.

Most beetles are carnivorous and hunt their prey. Both adults and larvae may have biting or chewing mouthparts with strong mandibles. The long-snouted weevils live on plants and some can be harmful garden pests, damaging foliage, petals and buds. Large numbers of beetles are ground dwellers, living in the soil or amongst the leaf litter. Beetles form part of nature's clean-up squad. Dead animals, animal droppings, rotting wood and rubbish of all kinds play host to a variety of beetles.

Click beetle.

Cardinal beetle.

Grasshoppers and crickets

Grasshoppers are more likely to be heard than seen in the sunny summer garden – until they suddenly jump. The buzzing song or stridulation (sounding like a sewing machine) of a grasshopper is created when the animal rubs its hindlegs against its wings.

Crickets don't usually start singing until the evening, and then carry on after dark. Be careful of the great green bush-cricket – it can bite you quite painfully.

Below: A speckled bush-cricket.

Above: A grasshopper.

Dragonflies and damselflies

Dragonflies, and the smaller, daintier, weak-flying damselflies, seem most active in the sunshine, which enhances their rich colours.

The major part of a dragonfly's life cycle is spent in water. The eggs are laid in water, where they develop into aquatic nymphs. Some species remain in that form for up to five years before crawling up a plant stem to emerge as adult dragonflies or damselflies. Most species then remain near the water although some are found well away from it.

The nymphs are ravenous hunters in the water, consuming tadpoles and other creatures. Adult dragonflies are dramatic and extremely agile flying predators that catch their insect prey in mid-air. They endlessly fly up and down their beat beside a stream or along a hedgerow or garden path or perch and then suddenly dart out at passing prey. These darters often perch on the page you are reading or on your arm in a very friendly fashion, dashing off briefly before returning to their station again.

Broad-bodied chaser dragonfly.

Common darter dragonfly.

Common blue damselfly.

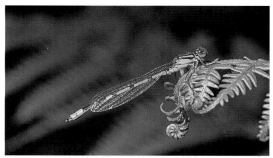

Azure damselfly.

Worms

There are probably more worms in your garden than you imagine. An acre of grassland might be home to three million earthworms! Worms are important allies in the garden, playing a vital part in recycling nutrients in the soil and maintaining its fertility. They are also a rich source of animal protein for members of the thrush family (including blackbirds and robins) and a major part of the diet of badgers. Brandling worms in particular love compost heaps and leaf piles, and some local councils are now offering householders 'wormeries' as a means of recycling organic kitchen and garden waste.

British earthworms may be under increasing threat from a foreign invader – the New Zealand flatworm. The 15cm (6in) flatworm coils its body around its earthworm prey and releases a powerful chemical that reduces the hapless earthworm to a soup that the flatworm can digest. The flatworm was probably introduced into Britain in soil on the roots of imported plants. First spotted in Northern Ireland and then in Scotland, the flatworm has no natural enemies and is spreading southwards. If it becomes widespread the consequences for soil fertility and for those animals that rely on earthworms for food could be dire.

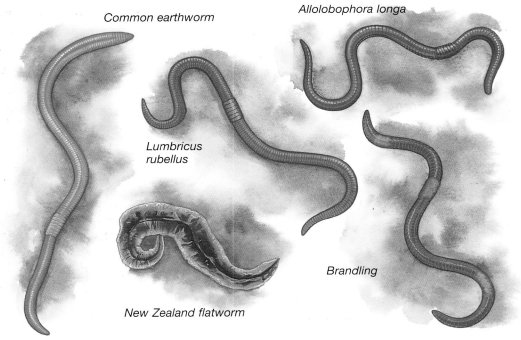

Common earthworm

Allolobophora longa

Lumbricus rubellus

Brandling

New Zealand flatworm

Spiders

All spiders are predators on invertebrates, immobilising their prey with poisoned fangs before sucking out the juices. None of Britain's native spiders has sufficient venom to harm humans or their pets.

WEBSPINNERS

There are several species of web-spinning house spiders, including the big, long-legged *Tegenaria gigantea*. Females can live for several years and can survive for months without water or food. Their cobwebs are triangular sheets in quiet corners of buildings, usually with an inbuilt tube as a retreat for the spider. You are most likely to notice house spiders in the autumn, when the more slender males are looking for a mate.

The most familiar outdoor web-spinner is the garden spider, with the characteristic white cross on its back and its elegant cartwheel web. A spiral web across your window frame has probably been made by a Zygiella species, which is also responsible for those little yellow cocoons under window ledges. The webs of the Linyphia family of spiders become dew-spangled hammocks on autumn hedges and the money spiders spread their sheets over the grass.

HUNTERS

The easily recognised little zebra spider, with its black-and-white stripes, is an expert jumper and can pounce on its prey from quite a long way.

Crab spiders are round-bodied little animals that ambush their prey, rather than spinning a web. They often lie in wait in a flower of their own colour. If you disturb one it will scuttle off sideways like a crab, hence their name.

Wolf spiders actively hunt their prey. If you look closely you can see their large eyes. You might see them sunbathing on a stone during the day, but they quickly disappear if disturbed. Some of the females carry their eggs in sacs or cocoons attached to their bodies.

Harvestmen are long-legged, tiny-bodied arachnids that are usually noticeable in late summer and sometimes find their way indoors. They are active at night and they eat insects and plant material; they also scavenge on carrion.

A garden spider eating a crane fly.

WHICH SPIDER?

Spiders are not insects: they are arachnids, a class of animals to which scorpions, ticks and mites also belong. Spiders can be easily distinguished from insects because they all have eight legs, whereas insects have six, and spiders do not have wings or antennae as insects do. Some spiders have wonderful colours and patterns. You could spend an interesting and instructive time getting to know the habits of a few of the multitude of spiders that inhabit your garden.

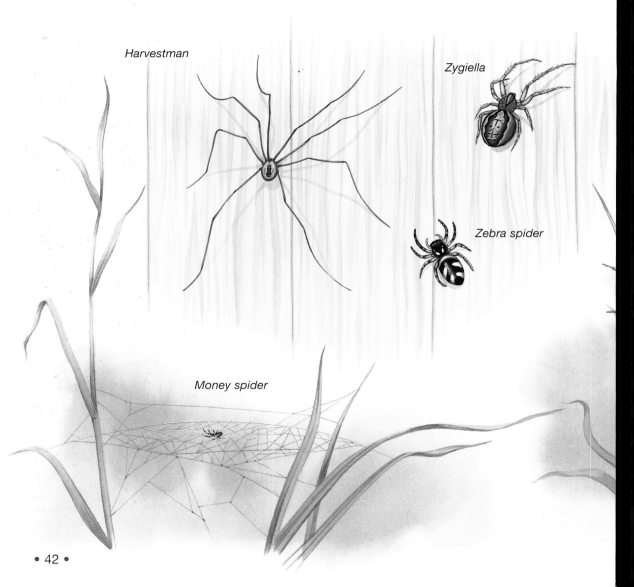

Harvestman

Zygiella

Zebra spider

Money spider

Close-up of garden spider in its web.

Tegenaria

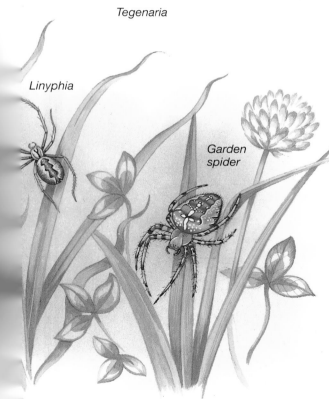

Linyphia

*Garden
spider*

*Female wolf spider carrying her eggs around in a
silk ball.*

Crab spider eating a honey bee.

Grubs

As you dig the garden, you often find grubs, which are insect larvae, in the soil. Some of them damage plants but they are essential links in the food chain, providing food for other wildlife, including mammals.

The cockchafer grub (which can be a serious destroyer of plant roots) will turn into what is also known as a May-bug: a big flying beetle that thuds loudly against windows when the lights are on.

FAT 'SNAKES'

Several species of hawkmoth caterpillar can be enormous and alarm many people but they are quite harmless. They are sometimes seen marching urgently in search of a good place to burrow into and pupate. They often have slanted stripes; some have mock 'eyes', and many have a 'horn' sticking up at the back – but it is not a sting and they cannot hurt you, though the caterpillar might 'threaten' you by rearing up at the front end.

Grubs look so different from the adults that it can be difficult to guess which are which. Here are some of the more common, shown with the adults.

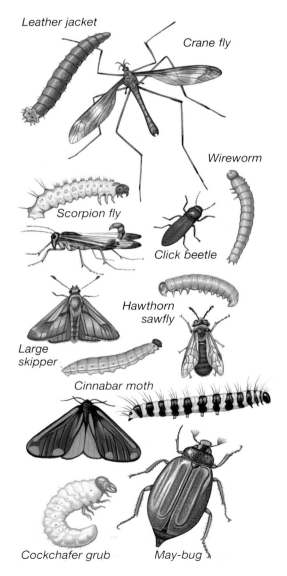

Leather jacket

Crane fly

Wireworm

Scorpion fly

Click beetle

Hawthorn sawfly

Large skipper

Cinnabar moth

Cockchafer grub

May-bug

The larva of the privet hawkmoth.

Slugs and snails

Some of these invertebrates are carnivores and prey on earthworms. The majority eat just about anything, and a few species go for your garden greenery in a big way.

Snails are an important food for thrushes; they are also eaten by blackbirds, ducks, hedgehogs, toads, frogs and slow-worms, which actually prefer slugs and take them in substantial numbers. You could help the thrushes by making sure they have plenty of stone 'anvils' in the garden to bash the snail shells on.

Snails are a food source for a great many garden visitors.

KIND CONTROL

If you really cannot tolerate your garden's slugs and snails, there are ways of deterring them or destroying them that will not inject poisons into the food chain or harm other species.

Take a torch into the garden at night, especially in damp weather when slugs and snails are most evident. You can then pick them off your plants.

Surround plants with materials that the creatures will find uncomfortable to crawl over – such as cinders, gorse trimmings, holly leaves, prickly butcher's broom leaves, ground-up egg-shells or fine sand. Use cut-down plastic drink bottles as mini-cloches.

Attract them to daytime resting places: they like to hide under planks, bits of old carpet and so on, or trap them by putting out scooped-out grapefruit halves (after you've eaten the fruit). But then you will have to dispose of live slugs – preferably not by throwing them into next door's garden!

Alternatively, let slugs die happily by drowning in a shallow bowl of beer.

Aphids

These tiny, swarming, sap-sucking bugs can give birth to active young several times a day! They can wreak havoc on selected plant species. Essentially they are after the plant sap, which they suck out by means of a needle-like tube, similar to the mouthparts that related bugs, such as fleas and lice, use to suck animal blood. The sap is very rich in sugar, which is excreted by the aphids as a waste product (they are really after the plant's protein) in the form of very sticky honeydew. This is a good source of food for ants, bees and other insects.

Aphids are also an excellent source of protein for a wide range of wildlife, especially nestlings, for which they can be vital. Thus the wildlife gardener is in a quandary regarding aphids: their presence will encourage birds into your garden but too many of the insects will spell trouble in the vegetable patch and on the roses and certain other plants. The art is to achieve a balance and let the rest of the wildlife deal with the aphids on your behalf as far as possible.

If you really cannot bear to live with aphids, do not use chemicals to kill them. They may well also kill beneficial insects and, with so many birds and other animals feeding on the aphids anyway, you risk denying a valuable food source to the animals you do want to attract.

An ant 'milking' aphids for their honeydew.

THE NIGHT GARDEN

An ultraviolet light will attract huge numbers of night-flying garden moths and you will be intrigued by their great variety. However, bats will also be drawn to investigate the display and you could end up with a lot of moth-wings and little else if you use 'lamping'.

Glow-worms are a type of beetle. Female glow-worms (which do the greenish glowing) have no wings and look more like larvae than adult beetles. It is the males of the related fireflies that flash as they fly in order to locate female fireflies, who perch on vegetation and flash back in response. The larvae of both fireflies and glow-worms eat snails.

The night garden will be alive with many other species of beetle, as well as slugs and snails, centipedes and millipedes, woodlice, many spiders and, in summer, the chirruping of crickets.

Female glow-worms flash to attract the low-flying males.

GARDENER'S HELPERS

Several insects are emphatically the gardener's friends and should be made very welcome indeed – including (sometimes especially) their generally nondescript larvae, which might easily be mistaken for 'pest' grubs. A ladybird will lay her eggs near a promising greenfly colony so the rapacious larvae can get to work as soon as they hatch. A single hoverfly larva can munch its way through 800 aphids in a fortnight.

LADYBIRDS AND LACEWINGS

Most ladybirds are carnivores, both adults and larvae. Look closely at these flying beetles and you will discover that there are several species, with differences in colour (yellows, reds and blacks) and the number and pattern of their spots. In seasons when ladybirds are exceptionally prolific they have been reported as biting humans, though in fact they are probably simply seeking moisture from sweat. The 'bite' is little more than a tiny irritation.

Lacewing larvae are similar in their appetites and not all that different from ladybird larvae to look at. The adults, however, are delicately winged, fragile-looking insects with green or brown bodies. The most widespread garden species (which tends to be nocturnal) is usually green but gradually becomes a light pinkish colour in autumn just before it hibernates. Lacewings and ladybirds both hibernate, and will often choose sheds, outhouses, lofts or come into the house.

A pair of twenty-two spot ladybirds.

A green lacewing resting on a leaf.

HOVERFLIES

These striped insects resemble wasps or bees but they don't buzz and they have no sting. These are the ones that keep company with you, hovering quietly at head level when you sit in the sun on their 'patch'. The hovering and flying style is quite unlike that of wasps and bees: they dart away every now and then but quickly return to their beat, maintaining the same position like a rescue helicopter over a shipwreck. The main food of the adult flies is nectar, especially from plants such as cow parsley and from blackberry flowers. The larvae of many hoverflies eat aphids.

CENTIPEDES AND MILLIPEDES

The helpful centipedes and the less helpful millipedes, both of which are long and many-legged, have very different roles. Both groups need damp habitats and avoid the light, preferring to emerge only at night, but they are not closely related animals.

Centipedes are predators, with 'claws' wrapped on either side of the head. The native species cannot harm you, though they might well try to bite if picked up and can give you a slight tingle. They move very fast and are light reddish-brown or ginger in colour. They can be useful to the gardener as they attack all sorts of other invertebrates.

Millipedes move slowly and eat plant matter (living as well as dead). Some species coil up when threatened and as a means of self-defence they can secrete a mixture of chemicals. This might stain your fingers if you pick up one of these animals but it won't hurt you.

Centipede

Millipede

Are they dangerous?

Many of the invertebrates perceived as pests or as scary or 'dangerous' are actually harmless or in fact positively beneficial to humans, to other wildlife and to gardens in general. Don't be fooled by appearances such as wasp-like stripes or apparent 'stings' and 'pincers'.

DISGUISES

The stripes on a wasp or a bee are a genuine warning that these insects are capable of defending themselves. Very often, however, the stripes are simply a ploy to warn off potential predators. The insect actually has no means of defence but by mimicking one, such as a wasp, that actually does have a sting the harmless insect tricks an attacker by appearing as if it too might sting. For example, the wasp-striped hoverflies, which are highly beneficial to the gardener, are quite harmless, as is the very wasp-like horntail or giant wood wasp. There are many other pretend stripeys in the garden.

FALSE BITERS

The 'pincers' at the tail-end of earwigs might be used by males to grab females during mating but you'll hardly feel it if they pinch you; the antler-like jaws of the stag beetle are used in fights between males, but not to bite humans. Weevils have a long snout with jaws at the end but they are essentially vegetarian and will not bite you, though they will wreak havoc with stored grain, flour and nuts or chew patterns out of the edges of your pea leaves.

Adult hoverflies are harmless nectar feeders and do not have stings.

A stag beetle's formidable-looking pincers are only used in fights between male beetles.

FALSE STINGERS

A real sting is usually not visible until the insect needs to use it. Usually what looks like an obvious sting in the tail is actually the insect's ovipositor, or egg-laying tube, which is used to place its tiny eggs in inaccessible hiding places. Typical of these non-stingers are the snakeflies (which seem to rear their heads like cobras) and the slender-waisted ichneumon wasps, which often add to the deception by being striped. Ichneumon wasps are parasites. Their larvae live on the young of other insects, especially caterpillars. You might feel just a tiny prick if you pick one up but it can't do you any real harm. There are also insects that imitate scorpions, with

The harmless ichneumon's long 'stinger' is in fact used for egg laying.

vicious-looking tails held erect, but again they are generally harmless – for example, the shade-loving scorpionfly and the devil's coach-horse.

WHY 'EARWIG'?

Do earwigs go into people's ears? It is most unlikely that they do, though they do spend the daylight hours safely tucked into small crevices, under bark, or perhaps hiding amongst the petals of a dahlia. They really do very little damage to the flowers and will happily move into a comfortable little earwig trap instead. Put a bamboo cane near the flowers with a small inverted flower pot full of straw on top.

(That might be a clue as to why people think earwigs like getting into ears: it goes back to the days when people slept on straw mattresses.)

REAL STINGERS AND BITERS

Invertebrates that really might sting humans or pets (usually in self-defence) include common wasps, hornets, honey bees and red ants.

Biters (essentially blood-suckers) are mosquitoes, biting midges, clegs, horse flies (*right*) and the common gnat.

Stings are actually modified ovipositors, so you will only be stung by a female, if that is any consolation, and she won't sting you unless provoked.

STUNG?

If a pet or a human does get stung, act quickly to minimise the discomfort. Honey bees usually leave their barbed stings in your skin, along with a little sac of venom. Be very careful not to grab hold of or squeeze the sac as it will simply empty more venom into you: try to scrape the sting gently away.

Antihistamines administered by a doctor will reduce your body's reaction to a sting in severe cases. In an emergency at home use acid for wasp stings (for example vinegar) and alkali for bee stings (for example soap).

With pets – especially inquisitive dogs – the greatest danger is in swallowing a stinging insect, which could result in the pet being stung in the throat, rendering it unable to breathe. In such cases get veterinary help immediately.

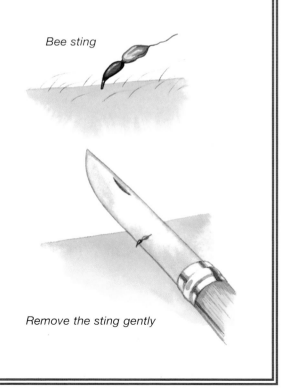

Bee sting

Remove the sting gently

GREEN PEST CONTROL

You can encourage the insects that eat your 'pests'. Wasp and hoverfly larvae, ladybirds (*above*) and lacewings and their larvae eat countless aphids. Centipedes eat various soil insects and small slugs. Ground beetles prey on cutworms and leatherjackets. Hoverflies can be attracted to your garden by growing, say, pot marigolds, which will also attract the parasitic wasps that attack cabbage-eating caterpillars.

Certain plants can help in your battle. Try 'companion planting' by sowing strong-smelling plants like tomato or wormwood, which will probably deter the whites, between your rows of cabbages. Growing a couple of rows of onions either side of a row of carrots will deter carrot fly.

Keep over-wintering host plants well away from your crops. Blackfly eggs are laid in autumn on shrubs like syringa, viburnum and spindle.

Use your hands! You can pick the yellow eggs or caterpillars of large white and small white butterflies off your vegetables, for example. And pinching out the growing tips of broad bean plants is a safe way of dealing with blackfly.

Pinching out an affected tip.

Traditional methods of preparing natural pesticides from extracts of rhubarb and elder leaves are actually illegal under current legislation. Commercially available organic pest sprays are not without their problems. Pyrethrum, for example, can kill ladybirds, bees and hoverflies as well as undesirables and will also harm fish, frogs and toads if it gets into your pond water. Derris is also lethal for fish, amphibians and reptiles in the garden.

Garden Ponds

If you want to attract and help to conserve a wide range of wildlife in your garden, then one of the best things to do is to make a wildlife pond. If you include plants of different species and growth-types, and ensure that the pond also offers a choice of water depths, including boggy areas, the pond can offer the widest possible variety of habitats.

Here are some of the main points you need to consider when planning a wildlife garden pond:

- where is your garden?
- what sort of wildlife thrives naturally in local conditions?
- can it reach the pond, and will it want to?
- where will the pond be?

SITING THE POND

Site the pond to suit the wildlife. How does its position relate to other wildlife habitats in or around the garden? Is it largely undisturbed by the presence and activities of humans (including neighbours) and pets?

Consider how much sunshine will fall on the pond. There should be much more sun than shade. Aim to keep the south side of the pond open to the sun. Include floating plants to give localised shade and shelter for the aquatic creatures that seek it.

Keep the pond well away from deciduous trees, which will choke it with leaves in the autumn. However, a certain amount of tree debris can offer habitats for a wide range of plants and invertebrates. Dead leaves can offer food for detritivores, organisms that eat the remains of dead plants and animals; and a broken branch lying in a pond big enough to accommodate it easily will soon be colonised by algae and invertebrates, some of which will utilise the fallen branch as a site for egg-laying.

The tranquillity of a garden pond in winter.

Designing the surroundings

The immediate surroundings of the pond should vary gradually, from water to damp margins to dry land. Build a short stretch of hard standing but make sure that there is a good strip of roughish grass leading up to the edge of the pond linking it with other habitats so that wildlife can travel to it safely.

Have some shrubs and ground-cover plants nearby where wildlife can shelter and hibernate, and build a rough rockery so that amphibians can pass the winter safely under the stones. Have a planted area of bog along one edge of the pond.

Remember that ponds receive run-off in the form of rainwater and this will carry substances used in the garden such as fertilisers, pesticides, path salt and creosote into the pond. Create a buffer zone around the pond to protect it from such pollution.

Don't make the edges of your pond too neat. Leave rough patches to give wildlife security.

What shape and size of pond?

If you want to attract the greatest variety of species, then the bigger and more diverse the pond the better. If you have a very big garden, a series of linked ponds, each offering different habitats to suit different species, would be ideal. However, anything is better than nothing and a useful minimum area for wildlife would be a pond of around 2.5 metres by 2 metres (about 9 feet long and 6 feet across).

The three-dimensional profile of the pond is far more important than the surface shape. Offer a variety of slopes and depths. Have very gentle slopes in at least part of the pond so that emerging young amphibians, insects or even ducklings can easily leave the water. These ramps will also be used by careless hedgehogs and small mammals which didn't really mean to go for a swim.

Provide shallows in some parts but also deep places (at least 75cm/30in deep) where the water will not freeze solid in winter, so that hibernating creatures have a chance to survive.

Have shelves in the water: frogs prefer to spawn at a depth of about 10cm (4in), natterjack toads spawn at 15cm (6in) or less, and common toads at 20 to 30cm (8 to 12in) deep. Marginal plants need shelves about 30cm (12in) deep. Make sure also that there is a suitable area for garden birds to drink and bathe.

Filling the pond

Natural ponds fill with rainwater or spring-water, but most garden ponds are initially filled with tap-water and this can cause problems as the water has invariably been treated with various additives. Leave your newly-filled pond for at least a week, to settle and lose its chlorine, before planting up.

In summer, top up the pond with rainwater from a garden butt if the level falls to less than about half its usual depth. Do this very gradually (which is always the key to successful wildlife pond management) and trickle the water in over a long period.

Planting up

The aim in planting a wildlife pond should be practical rather than aesthetic, though the two need not be incompatible. Plants are the basis of a good pond, providing oxygen, food, refuges, egg-laying sites, hatching sites and a great deal more for the wildlife you want to attract.

Choose native plant species in preference to imported varieties. Aim for diversity, not only in species, but also in the densities at which they are planted (thick growth in some parts, open water in others). You will also need to maintain a balance between the main groups of plants in your pond.

Try to include:

- submerged plants to oxygenate the water;
- plants with floating leaves, to shade out algae and provide shelter, egg-laying sites and food for larvae;
- plants that emerge from the water and stand up from the plant-shelves at the edge of the pond and in the boggy area (ideal as sites for emerging dragonfly larvae).

The choice of species will depend partly on what thrives in local conditions. If native plants find their way into your pond don't treat them like invading weeds, but welcome them.

ALGAE

Algae are important food sources and habitats for some creatures, but if the algal cover on your garden pond becomes excessive it will lead to a lack of oxygen in the water, which benefits nothing except some types of bacteria.

There is often a big build-up of algae in a pond's first year, until other plants and animals become well enough established to create a good balance and keep the algae in check. Mats of slimy blanketweed covering the pond would suggest over-enrichment of the water. This might occur if, for example, manure or fertiliser has washed into the pond.

Do not apply chemicals to kill the algae. Freshwater crustaceans, such as Daphnia, eat algae, and shade from larger plants and trees over some parts of the pond can discourage the seasonal algal 'blooms'. You can rake out the mats in late autumn, but take care, you will also be raking out plenty of animal life. Remove a small area of algae at a time and leave it on the bank overnight to give animals a chance to return to the pond. Then put the stuff on the compost heap.

Introducing wildlife

Leave the plants to establish themselves for a year before you introduce animal life, as it might overwhelm very young plants. By then you will find that quite a few invertebrates, such as dragonflies and various water bugs and beetles, have made their own way into your pond.

Great diving beetles are good fliers and will find your pond if they are in the area. They prefer weedy ponds. These big reddish-brown, yellow-bordered beetles are excellent swimmers and ferocious hunters: they attack invertebrates, fish, tadpoles (up to 20 a day per beetle) and even adult frogs and newts. Adult great silver beetles, which look silvery in the water, are vegetarian and browse on water weeds, although the favourite food of their larvae are water snails.

Whirligig beetles, which whirl around on the water surface, are much smaller. The adults will take small insects that have fallen into the water, while the larvae prey on mosquito larvae. Screech beetles, which inhabit muddy ponds and prey on invertebrates, squeak when they are alarmed.

For the sake of the wildlife, do not put fish in your pond – and certainly do not introduce alien species such as goldfish, which will simply devour all your invertebrates and tadpoles.

Common frogs among duckweed.

Close up of hornwort in pond.

Predators

A wide variety of predators might prey on your pondlife, including:

- herons on fish. These are marvellous birds to watch, but if they habitually deplete your pond of fish you will have to devise a wire-mesh cover that they cannot penetrate but that does not impede pond residents. Herons will also take amphibians, reptiles, insects and small mammals;
- cats;
- grass snakes on fish, amphibians and reptiles.

Tadpoles are a food source for many animals and are eaten by water beetles and their larvae, greater water boatmen, also known as back-swimmers (which might also bite your finger), dragonfly nymphs, water scorpions, fish, newts, water shrews and ducks.

The bigger the pond, the more chance its inhabitants have of finding shelter and avoiding predators.

Let smaller invertebrates become established before deliberately introducing larger creatures that might eat them. With permission from the landowner, collect pondweed or even just pond water and pond mud locally: it will already contain a variety of invertebrates. Carefully selected native species of mollusc will help to keep the water clean.

Do not try to stock your pond with adult frogs and toads: you might be introducing disease and they will, in any case, wander off and probably get squashed or eaten. Newts might stay, given company of their own kind. Also be wary of importing spawn, because of the risk of disease.

Above: A cat is attracted by spawning frogs.

Right: A heron on the lookout for a meal.

Reptiles and Amphibians

British gardens are not rich in reptiles and amphibians. If you are lucky you might come across a toad on a damp garden path at night, or a tiny, copper-eyed lizard sunbathing on a stone during the day, or perhaps be startled when a frog suddenly sprints across the grass in a series of hops. But only those with suitable ponds might be homes for newts, and few gardens are honoured by visits from snakes.

Unlike birds and mammals, reptiles and amphibians cannot produce internal heat from digesting their food. Instead, they have to absorb external warmth and they do so by basking in the sun. Because of this, this group of animals is sometimes described as 'cold-blooded', though in fact their body temperatures, when they are active, might be as warm as yours.

PROTECTED SPECIES

Several species of reptiles and amphibians have declined in numbers recently, even some of the more common ones, and some are threatened with extinction locally. In most cases this can be attributed to the loss of natural habitats, which is why it is so important that these animals should be made welcome in gardens. The introduction of ponds in many gardens, for example, may have helped offset the losses brought about by the filling in of larger ponds on farmland.

Under the Wildlife and Countryside Act 1981 the great crested newt, natterjack toad, sand lizard and smooth snake are fully protected in Britain. It is also an offence to kill, injure or sell grass snakes, adders, slow-worms or common lizards, and there are restrictions on the sale of other newts and the common frog and toad.

The slow-worm is neither a worm nor a snake, as its appearance might suggest. It is a harmless, legless lizard.

A male sand lizard resplendent in his late-spring breeding colours. The males will fight fierce battles for the privilege of pairing with a female.

ALIENS

Several exotic species of reptile and amphibian have escaped, or been deliberately released by pet-owners, and some are beginning to live quite happily in the wild. The edible frog, marsh frog, wall lizard and green lizard have all established breeding colonies. Pet turtles and tortoises are also sometimes 'lost' or released into the wild and could find their way into your garden.

The marsh frog is the largest of the European frogs, measuring up to 12.5cm (5in) long. It was introduced to Britain in 1935 and has since become established in Kent and Sussex.

REPTILE OR AMPHIBIAN?

Reptiles have dry skins with scales. They are primarily land animals (though some species swim in search of prey) and they do not need water for mating or for their young. Native British reptiles include three species of snake and three lizards.

Amphibians have bare, moist skin. They breed in water. Their eggs wither if they are not kept moist, so the females lay their eggs in ponds. The newly hatched young are called tadpoles and live in the water. They breathe through gills, like fish. Native British amphibians include one frog, two toads and three newts.

Sand lizard

Female great crested newt

GRASS SNAKE (1)
More common in south than north; absent from Scotland. Lives near water (fast swimmer) and can climb trees. Olive green with characteristic yellow collar. Eyes with round pupil. Britain's largest snake: females can grow to 120cm (4 feet) or more.

ADDER (2)
Widespread but rather localised. Characteristic darker zigzag pattern on thick grey-brown body. Small eyes with vertical pupil. 50–60cm (19½–23in).

SMOOTH SNAKE (3)
Very local and very rare. Heathland and open woodland; good climber. Dark stripe from mouth across eye and along neck. Brown to brownish-grey with black stippling. Slender body. 55–70cm (21½–27in).

SLOW-WORM (4)
Widespread: woods, forest edge, meadows, moist heathland, clumpy grass, banks. Legless lizard, long and slender; greyish to coppery brown; smooth scales, moveable eyelids. 30–50cm (12–19½in).

COMMON LIZARD (5)
Widespread, not fussy about habitat. Dainty; brown-grey or dark olive; brown and black markings. 10–15cm (4–6in).

SAND LIZARD (6)
Very local; endangered. Sand dunes, sandy heaths – likes very varied vegetation structure. Sturdy. Green or light brown with dark markings. 15–20cm (6–8in).

COMMON FROG (7)
Widespread in damp habitats. Yellow/green or brown/grey with reddish or brown markings. Agile: tends to hop. 7–9cm (2½–3½in).

COMMON TOAD (8)
Widespread. Rough 'warty' brown skin; squat and plump. Reluctant to move, tends to crawl rather than hop. 8–10cm (3–4in).

NATTERJACK TOAD (9)
Rare and very local — mainly coastal dunes and sandy heaths. Olive brown/green with red and grey markings and characteristic yellow stripe along back. Runs or walks. 6–8cm (2–3in).

SMOOTH (COMMON) NEWT (10)
Widespread in lowlands, preferring damp spots with some sunlit areas. Olive green/brown, spotted belly. 7–10cm (2½–4in).

PALMATE NEWT (11)
Common on heaths and mountains; scarce in the Midlands and East Anglia. Will use any small pool for breeding — even a puddle. Webbed hindfeet. Small; olive brown, green spots. 7–9cm (2½–3½in).

GREAT CRESTED (WARTY) NEWT (12)
Widespread, but not common, in larger ponds with good plant growth. Warty skin, dark grey/brown; males crested in breeding season. 12–16cm (4½–6in).

REPTILE LIFE CYCLES

Reptiles usually mate in the spring, once the temperature has reached 13–15°C (55–59°F).

The common lizard gives birth to fully-developed young, as do adders, smooth snakes and slow-worms. The young, usually about half a dozen of them, are born in the summer or early autumn.

Grass snakes and sand lizards lay eggs. The grass snake lays as many as 40 white, leathery eggs around June in somewhere warm and humid, such as a compost heap or under rotting logs or down a mammal's burrow. The eggs hatch in late summer. The sand lizard lays her few eggs in a sandy burrow.

Slow-worms have a pregnancy that lasts at least a year; in other species it is 10–12 weeks.

Reptiles will not breed until they are anything from two to four years old, depending on species and on sex. The great majority of them will perish before having the opportunity to breed.

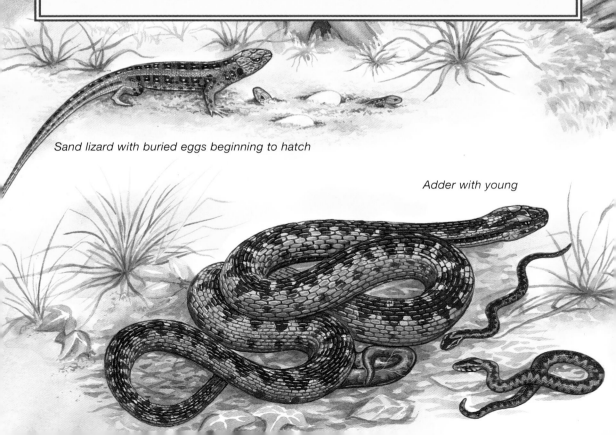

Sand lizard with buried eggs beginning to hatch

Adder with young

Common lizard with young

Grass snake with eggs beginning to hatch

Amphibian life cycles

Frogs might start migrating towards their breeding sites as early as January, at night, in mild, damp weather. Common toads are on the move several weeks later, mostly by night, building up to huge numbers. Natterjack toads move in small groups at night around April over a long period. Newts migrate to their ponds in early spring.

Frog and toad mating ponds are a seething mass of activity. Frogs usually mate after dark, with much croaking, splashing and fighting. The actual egg-laying usually taking place around three in the morning. Common toads mate night and day. Natterjack males croak so loudly that you can hear them from quite a distance in late spring and early summer.

Each frog lays a clump of up to 3,000 eggs, and the clumps all stick together to form large mats of spawn. Each common toad lays 800 to 2,500 eggs, in double-rowed strings attached to plants. Natterjacks lay a similar number of eggs but in single-row strings.

The courtship of newts is more leisurely, with elaborate displays by the males. They lay only 200–300 eggs, each one individually wrapped in or on a leaf.

Amphibians take up to four years to reach sexual maturity.

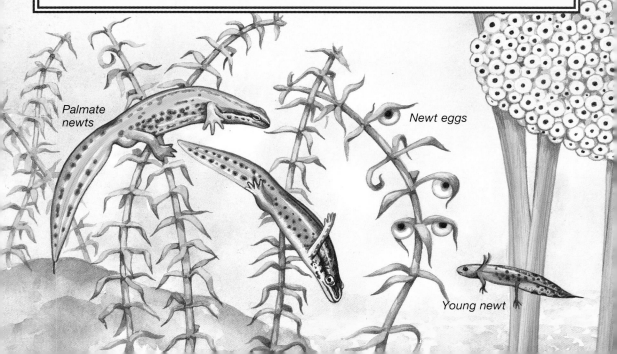

Palmate newts

Newt eggs

Young newt

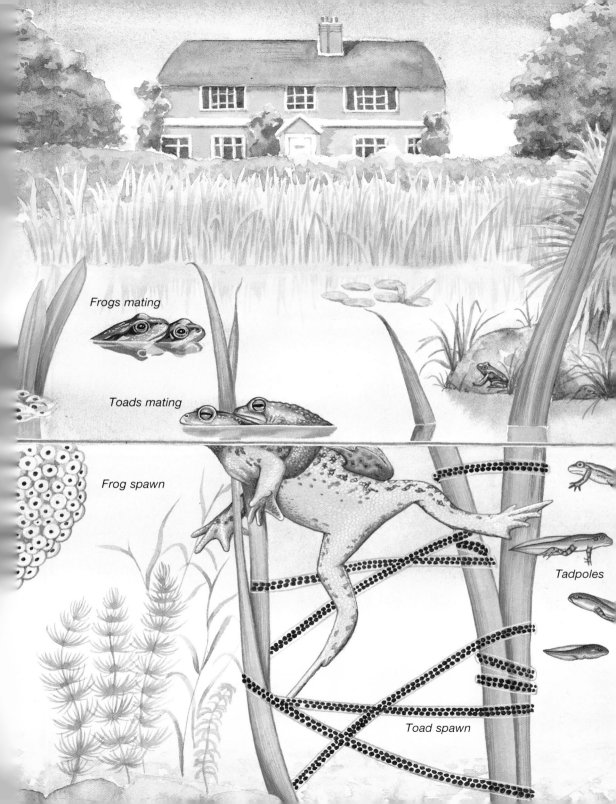

Frogs mating

Toads mating

Frog spawn

Tadpoles

Toad spawn

TADPOLES

Frog tadpoles are brownish with gold specks; toad tadpoles are jet black. Neither looks anything like the parents. Newt tadpoles look very much like miniature adults, complete with legs and tails, except that they have feathery gills. Frog and toad tadpoles are omnivorous; they eat pond plants and pond animals (including other, weaker tadpoles). Newt tadpoles eat a wide range of small aquatic animals.

Frog and toad tadpoles gradually acquire legs and lose their tails as they slowly metamorphose into adults. This takes about 12 weeks for the common frog and common toad, and six to eight weeks for the natterjack toad.

The very great majority of tadpoles are devoured by a wide range of aquatic invertebrates and fish. Newts, water shrews and ducks also take frog tadpoles, but not those of toads.

In midsummer the surviving tadpoles have become air-breathing frogs and toads and leave the water, all emerging on to the land over a matter of days (ideally in a downpour). Many are taken by thrushes and blackbirds; others fail to get out of the pond and drown (they no longer have gills to breathe with in water); others are baked to death by hot sun if they cannot find shelter. The survivors disperse, to grow and mature, returning to the pond to breed up to four years later, if they survive that long.

SPAWN-SHARING

Some people think they have too much spawn in their ponds, while others have an empty pond they are longing to stock with spawn. In general, exchanging spawn can be a bad idea, as there is a risk of introducing disease. Out of the thousands of eggs laid by each frog or toad, probably only five or six adults will survive to lay their own eggs. The loss to predators is extremely high. Remember this when you think that you have 'too much' spawn in your pond.

Two pairs of common frogs mate in a pond. Frogs will return year after year to breed in the same ponds. Because so many natural ponds have been filled in, drained or poisoned by chemicals, garden ponds provide vital alternative breeding areas for frogs and other amphibians.

What's for dinner?

All British reptiles and amphibians are carnivores and they take a very wide range of prey.

Grass snakes are good swimmers and eat amphibians and small fish; they might also take the occasional nestling, vole or mouse. Smooth snakes eat lizards, the young of other snakes, and a few nestlings, young shrews and mice. Adders prey mainly on short-tailed voles and mice. Young snakes of all species eat earthworms, insects, spiders and slugs.

Slow-worms choose slugs for preference but will also take earthworms, spiders, ants and caterpillars and occasionally baby rodents and reptiles. The other lizards concentrate on spiders, all sorts of insects, earthworms, woodlice, centipedes and a few slugs and snails.

Frogs and toads both devour slugs, snails, woodlice, beetles and other insects, earthworms, spiders, millipedes and centipedes, but avoid wasps and hairy caterpillars. Toads will also eat ants. Newts catch whatever they can in the water (although they avoid toad tadpoles); on land they emerge on damp nights to hunt for worms, grubs, beetles, crickets, slugs and snails.

A grass snake, emerging from a pond, stalks a common frog.

Are they dangerous?

None of the British species of reptile or amphibian is in the least dangerous to you, apart from the adder, our only venomous snake, and even then the risk is very slight. Adders do not attack without provocation, biting only in self-defence, usually if taken by surprise. The greatest risk of being bitten is when they are at their least alert, either just before or soon after hibernation. Their strike range is only about 15cm (6in) and they are certainly not going to chase after you to score a hit – quite the reverse. If you are worried, stamp as you walk: they are very sensitive to ground vibrations and will slide out of your way.

An adder's venom is only sufficient to kill its small prey and dogs and cats are unlikely to be seriously affected by an adder bite. However, if you suspect that your pet has been bitten it is wise to take it to the vet for examination. Humans usually suffer no more than localised swelling and some discomfort for a day or two. The risk of being bitten is tiny compared with the risk of being stung by bees or wasps, and the effect is often not much more severe. Between 1876 and 1976, only 14 people in Britain died following adder bites and they were probably particularly sensitive to the venom, as some people are to bee stings.

Adders are a protected species and it is illegal to kill or harm them (or any British snake).

If you have an adder in the garden it may possibly present a danger to very young children or foolish pets. Otherwise, treasure it and use the opportunity to get to know it. If you

ADDER BITES

If you are bitten by an adder:
- keep the bitten limb as still as possible;
- go to the nearest accident and emergency department as soon as possible;
- if a bite victim loses consciousness apply resuscitation if necessary and keep in the recovery position.

are really concerned, contact the RSPCA or your local wildlife trust for advice.

The usual self-defence of grass snakes is to vanish as fast as they can, usually very noisily. If caught, a grass snake will often 'play dead', or it will writhe furiously and bombard you with a foul-smelling liquid. It might hiss and mock-strike but it can't hurt you. Smooth snakes are docile but will 'bite' if really provoked, especially if squeezed, though they have no venom.

Slow-worms were often pets for country children and are generally very affable. Their main means of defence is autotomy, which means that, like other

If it is threatened, a grass snake may pretend to be dead until a predator loses interest in it.

lizards, they can shed their tails to escape. If you grab the tail of a slow-worm, that is all you are left with.

None of Britain's amphibians are dangerous. The common frog's only defence is agility. The common toad relies initially on camouflage (which is why it does not get out of the way of your strimmer). Toads don't seem to mind being handled gently by humans. A toad might empty its bladder if startled, producing a harmless liquid

with a faint odour. No toad tolerates being squeezed and will employ its greatest defence, its body warts, which can produce a sticky white excretion. A dog with a mouthful of toad will immediately froth at the mouth and spit out the toad. Although the dog might vomit and perhaps experience local paralysis for a while, it will not become really ill – but it will have learnt its lesson. Crested newts also have warty skins that produce noxious excretions to put off predators.

Don't worry about getting warts from a toad. Human warts are caused by a virus

A flower-pot is an ideal place for a common toad to sit in reasonable safety while it waits for its next meal to come by. Toads are frequently found in gardens and deeper ponds can provide them with valuable breeding places. Their warty secretions discourage predators, but won't harm you.

whereas a toad's 'warts' are glands for producing and secreting defensive toxins.

In the presence of its greatest enemy, a grass snake, a toad will inflate its body and stand on tiptoe so that it looks too big to be swallowed. It might do that to you, too.

Garden attractions

The reptile or amphibian species that might visit or reside in your garden depend on where you live and what conditions are like there.

Reptiles tend to move to different habitats according to the season. Most of them prefer dry heath or grassland. They are very shy of humans and other interference. In the garden they need:

- somewhere dry and sheltered for the winter;
- somewhere warm to feed and rest;
- somewhere sunny and undisturbed for basking;
- somewhere to shelter from the sun on very hot days;
- the right environment for their eggs (grass snake and sand lizard) or

- somewhere safe to give birth to live young;
- somewhere for the growing young to hide, such as overgrown ditches and pits, with suitable food;
- water for drinking.

Their ideal garden is large enough for them not to be disturbed and is preferably neglected, with patches of bare soil and short grass, and leaf litter lying about. A compost heap or an undisturbed woodpile will provide a supply of invertebrate food, somewhere to hide and somewhere for the egg-laying species to nest. A garden pond will attract grass snakes. Reptiles are quite happy to bask on undisturbed wasteland.

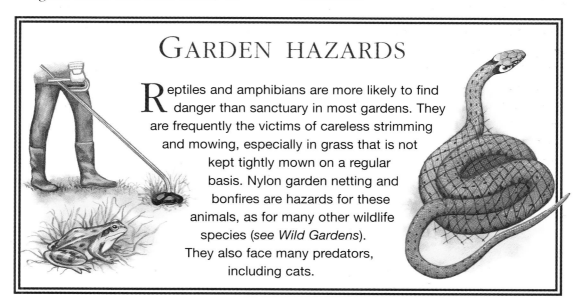

GARDEN HAZARDS

Reptiles and amphibians are more likely to find danger than sanctuary in most gardens. They are frequently the victims of careless strimming and mowing, especially in grass that is not kept tightly mown on a regular basis. Nylon garden netting and bonfires are hazards for these animals, as for many other wildlife species (see Wild Gardens). They also face many predators, including cats.

Amphibians must have access to water, particularly in the breeding season, though their breeding ponds might be several kilometres away from their habitat for the rest of the year. If you live on a new housing estate, you might be surprised in early spring by the arrival of armies of frogs or toads in search of a traditional breeding pond long since built over. Toads in particular are very faithful to these ponds and it is difficult to persuade a toad to use a new site as it will almost always head back to its traditional pond. Frogs are much more likely to colonise new ponds.

Frogs usually prefer smallish ponds but toads like larger ponds and lakes. However, a garden pond can offer either animal a good source of food even if they choose to go elsewhere for breeding. Frogs like dampish areas in the garden; toads favour a dry habitat, but both prefer to be undisturbed.

Whereas frogs and toads often spend much of the year a long way from water, newts definitely need ponds: they spend much more of their time in water than other amphibians and usually continue to live by their ponds as adults. Newts will make use of a good garden pond.

A well-designed and sited garden pond can provide a source of food and a place to breed for many reptiles and amphibians. It will also bring pleasure and fascination for wildlife watchers!

Winter survival

Reptiles and amphibians take steps to avoid the extremes of winter. They cannot remain active at low temperatures and could not easily survive the cold, cloudy winter days. Generally snakes head for their hibernation quarters around October, although they will sometimes move as early as late August if conditions are poor. Adders and smooth snakes retire to burrows or holes made by tree roots. Grass snakes also occupy wall crevices or hide beneath stones. Lizards similarly seek the shelter of cracks and stones. Most of them hide away from October to March but some adders and common lizards will emerge to bask on warm, sunny winter days.

Amphibians also hide from the cold during the winter months but you may come across a wandering toad in the garden on warm, moist nights during winter. It will be almost black – toads become very dark in winter. Toads and newts prefer dry quarters, sometimes common toads simply make themselves a little hole not very far into the soil, though natterjacks go deeper into soft sand. Newts hide under stones or logs. Frogs, especially males, might spend the winter underwater in the depths of a pond where the water doesn't freeze.

WINTER HELP

Make sure that your pond is suitable for any amphibians that might choose to spend the winter in its depths. Leave damp heaps undisturbed for frogs and newts that hibernate on land. Toads and newts might occupy the corner of a shed or a rockery – try not to disturb them. Always take care with winter gardening: there may be a toad under that pile of stones or simply in a hole in the soil where you are about to dig.

Common frogs hibernate through the winter months, finding shelter on muddy pond bottoms or hiding on land.

Newts usually hibernate on land in damp, sheltered spots, such as beneath fallen branches.

Birds

Imagine: great tits, blue tits, coal tits and marsh tits in your garden shrubs and trees, all waiting for a space on the nut hangers and bacon rinds. A noisy flock of greenfinches, chaffinches and sparrows squabble for the seed on the bird-table. Below, on the frosty grass, three robins have temporarily set aside their ferocious territorial disputes to tuck into brown, crumbly meal full of insects and honey or pick at breadcrumbs, grated cheese and suet.

Blackbird

The resident male blackbird has given up trying to chase off intruders and a few fieldfares and redwings are pecking at halved apples in company with a song thrush and a mistle thrush. A great spotted woodpecker lands on the nut cage, its sudden arrival scattering the tits and a nuthatch. Here and there in the garden linnets and goldfinches daintily probe teasel seedheads and investigate the withered, fluffy remains of michaelmas daisies and goldenrod.

It would be a well-favoured garden that was as enthusiastically visited as this, but the winter garden can certainly be alive with birds. Very often it is the winter birds that first spark people's interest in garden wildlife. Apart from supplementary winter feeding, what draws birds into gardens, even in the heart of urban areas?

Greenfinch

House sparrow

Goldfinch

Redwing

Berry-bearing trees are an excellent winter food source for garden birds.

Nuthatch

Chaffinch

Starling

Blue tit

Coal tit

Robin

Great tit

Fieldfare

Mistle thrush

Song thrush

Garden attractions

A bird looks for the usual essentials: food for all seasons, shelter, the chance of finding a mate and somewhere to raise young. To make your garden more attractive to birds, you need to provide:

- natural food at all times of the year, for the young as well as for adults (the young tend to need animal protein even when the parents are seed-eaters);
- supplementary feeding when necessary;
- water for drinking and bathing, all year round;
- natural nesting sites, supplemented if necessary with nesting-boxes carefully designed and sited to suit particular species;
- relative safety from predators.

The preferred garden for birds is mature and slightly scruffy with well-established trees and shrubs and plenty of variety in the way of herbaceous and other borders. There should be lots of native plant species, a vegetable patch, fruit areas, some lawn, 'wilderness' areas where nettles, thistles, groundsel and teasel are allowed to flourish and set their seed, ponds and puddles to provide water for drinking and bathing, thick hedges and outbuildings with nesting crannies, compost heaps, log piles, dead wood for fungi and insects, moss for nesting materials and not too much human activity.

The robin is one of the most familiar of garden visitors.

Planting for birds

Garden plants can provide direct benefits for birds in the shape of fruit and seeds for food, but above all they provide habitats for the invertebrates on which so many birds, especially their young, will feed. Around half of European bird species rely partly or entirely on invertebrates as their primary food source. Plantings can also be designed to provide safety and places where birds can forage among the leaf litter (don't clear up all the leaves in autumn), as well as potential nesting sites and song perches in bushes, hedges, climbers and trees.

A female blackbird finds food in a winter garden.

IVY

The native ivy is a most important plant for wildlife. It provides nectar for insects at a time when there is very little else; its berries are relished in early winter by pigeons and other birds; it offers marvellous hiding places and nesting if it is allowed to scramble into trees.

Ivy in a hawthorn tree is a wonderful combination for wildlife. Ignore tales of ivy strangling trees: it doesn't. A very substantial growth of ivy could shade out some of the tree's own leaves, or even eventually make it top-heavy and vulnerable to winter gales, but let it scramble up any already dead or dying trees in the garden, and over outbuildings and walls.

PLANTING A BRAND NEW GARDEN

Although a new garden will take time to mature, you can plant it up with birds in mind right from the start. Aim for variety and don't be too neat.

If you have the space for it in your garden (and it would have to be vast to accommodate all of these!) you might plant trees and shrubs to attract insects and provide spring nectar in their flowers and summer or autumn fruit. Those you might consider include native species such as oak, birch, hawthorn, goat or pussy willow and hazel; also ash, beech, hornbeam and alder for their seeds, and conifers (pine, spruce and larch) for cones enjoyed by finches. Holly, wild cherry, rowan, spindle and elder are excellent natives for fruit and, above all, crabs and

other apple trees for blossom and fruit. Your hedges might include blackthorn (sloe), yew and wild privet – but remember that clipping will deter them from flowering and fruiting. Berried shrubs include blackberry, elder, ivy, honeysuckle, cotoneaster, berberis, pyracantha and mahonia. Also plant hedges with a view to providing shelter and nesting sites. Evergreen hedges are invaluable for both purposes (try laurel as well as conifers). The hedges are a refuge for insects too.

Don't forget the wildlife when you plant your flowerbeds. Aubrieta, for example, is good for insects and provides seed for birds. Also consider pansies, snapdragons, teasel and a selection of weeds (some are attractive to people as well as insects

A jay 'anting'. Acid sprayed by the ants helps to kill parasites in the bird's feathers.

and birds). Leave the seedheads for finches to peck at during winter. Lawns can be important feeding grounds for birds with plenty of invertebrates in the grass and beneath it. Ants and their eggs are food for some (green woodpeckers in particular), and when ants emerge for their mass nuptial flight many birds take advantage of this sudden aerial bounty.

Sparrows having a dust bath.

A female blackbird sunning herself.

WATER

A supply of fresh water, for both drinking and bathing, is vital for birds at all times of the year. At the very least offer them an untippable bird-bath of some kind. Better still would be to incorporate a bird bathing and drinking area as part of a full-size wildlife pond. Even the smallest bird-bath should have sloping sides so that small birds can get in and out easily, and a deeper area (say 8cm/3in or more) for larger birds such as pigeons to have a good wallow. The surface should be rough enough not to be slippery underfoot. Site your bird-bath away from the bird-table (to avoid food and droppings contaminating it) and close enough to trees or large shrubs so that the birds have somewhere safe to preen and dry off after a bath.

Keep the bath clean by emptying it regularly and filling it with fresh water. In winter, keep the water ice-free: you can set the bath on bricks so that there is space underneath for a nightlight candle to take the chill out of the water, but avoid doing this with a fibre-glass bath!

A jay bathing. Feather care is of vital importance for birds.

What will I see?

Most gardens will support some fifteen to twenty species of bird, with another ten or so as visitors. Birds, with the advantage of flight, can move from one area to another with relative ease. According to the British Trust for Ornithology (BTO), the species most commonly seen in winter gardens countrywide during recent years have included:

Blackbird	House sparrow
Blue tit	Magpie
Chaffinch	Robin
Coal tit	Rook
Collared dove	Song thrush
Dunnock	Starling
Great tit	Woodpigeon
Greenfinch	Wren

Many other species are seen, of course – gulls in coastal gardens and moorhens and mallards near inland water, for example. Summer visitors, depending on location, might include warblers (garden warbler, chiffchaff, blackcap, willow warbler), spotted flycatcher, house martins, swallows and linnets. In winter you might see flocks of fieldfares and redwings and, especially during hard winters, bramblings and reed buntings. At any time of year birds of prey such as sparrowhawk and kestrel might be seen, and in rural areas the delightful day-flying little owl, which sometimes nests in hollow trees in undisturbed gardens.

A wood pigeon in an orchard.

Blackbird

♀

♂

Great spotted
woodpecker

♀

♂

House sparrow

♂

Greenfinch ♂

Blackcap ♂

♀

Chaffinch ♂

Differences between the sexes of
some common garden birds.

♂ = male
♀ = female

♀

Wren

Spotted
flycatcher

Linnet

Collared dove

Woodpigeon

Magpie

Dunnocks

Garden warbler

Starling in
summer plumage

Rook

Night birds

The nocturnal garden is full of life. Tawny owls might be seen, or more likely heard, even in urban gardens. Barn owls, which have rapidly declined in numbers as their rural habitats vanished or deteriorated, are not town birds. The silent, almost ghostly whitish creature floating along the hedgerows is unmistakable, and the long, blood-curdling shriek is quite unlike the familiar calls of the tawny owl. It is particularly unnerving when the bird decides to shout while sitting on top of your chimney-pot!

Night singers include two well-loved summer visitors, the nightjar and the nightingale, both again increasingly rare even in areas where they used to be numerous. Once heard, both are unforgettable: the nightingale has such a rich song (the blackcap might fool you in the daytime but it doesn't have the 'jug jug' phrase of the nightingale) and the nightjar makes an extraordinary churring sound.

At dusk most gardens are alive to the sound of blackbirds, and sometimes you might hear the strange creak of a woodcock as it flies fast and straight on patrol over its regular beat.

A barn owl in flight is an unforgettable sight.

Woodcock

Nightingale

Nightjar

Feeding garden birds

Birds can be grouped according to the type of food that they eat and it is important to know what to provide if you want to attract particular species to your garden. Basically, there are those that eat mainly invertebrates and those that eat seeds (including grain). You can usually tell by the shape of the beak: birds that probe crevices in search of insects have slender beaks, for example, while those that crack grain have stout, strong beaks.

SUPPLEMENTARY FEEDING

Garden feeding in winter has a huge impact on the populations of certain species, especially since agricultural practices have changed in recent years so that many birds have found much less to scavenge in the winter countryside.

In spring, many birds experience a 'hungry gap': weed-seeds, wild nuts and berries have long since been eaten, and insects are not yet available or may even have their emergence disrupted by late frosts or very heavy rain. Tits, for example, time their breeding season in order to coincide with the abundance of caterpillars, aphids, spiders and millipedes on which their nestlings depend. If these are not available, the nestlings will die. Therefore putting out

Garden birds need extra help in the winter.

seed and insectivore mix in May will help birds such as finches and tits.

In summer, long periods of drought might result in the ground being baked so hard that members of the thrush family (including blackbirds and robins) cannot dig invertebrates out of the soil. You can help by putting out suitable food for them, and you might also ensure that at least some part of the garden is thoroughly watered so that there is always somewhere where the soil is workable and the leaf litter is kept moist. Opening up a section of the compost heap will be greatly welcomed at any time of the year by this group of birds.

Garden feeding can help birds to bridge these difficult periods and a case can be made for offering supplementary food for garden birds at almost any time of the year. However, such feeding should be done with great care. It is particularly important that nestlings should be fed naturally by their parents: they need invertebrate protein in order to grow and develop properly. There is a serious risk that parents might try to feed their young on unsuitable food if the insect life is less than abundant. On no account give birds access to whole peanuts at this time of year or anything else that might choke the nestlings if popped into those gaping, greedy little beaks. Supplementary feeding at this time should really be directed at the busy parents only!

A well-stocked bird-table will attract a variety of visitors. These are blue and great tits.

HOW TO FEED

Regularity is important. Peak feeding times are dawn and midday. Beware of leaving food out late in the day, as it could be an invitation to rodents.

Where you put the food is just as important as what you feed. Scatter the food on the ground or put it on a bird-table; hang up food containers or place them on top of poles; stuff food into cracks in bark. Each method attracts different species. Ground-feeders include robin, blackbird, thrushes, chaffinch, dunnock, wren, pigeons and doves, pheasants, etc.; all except the last five will take food from a table as well as from the ground, but most are happier on the ground. Tits, nuthatches greenfinches and spotted woodpeckers

will use hanging food containers; other species (such as sparrows and starlings) learn to perch on these too. Good hygiene is essential. Scrub bird-tables and food containers regularly. Change ground feeding sites from time to time, to avoid build-up of disease. Beware of musty peanuts and only buy those guaranteed free from aflatoxins.

The wren will not take food from bird-tables or other bird feeders.

The most difficult garden bird to help is the tiny, secretive wren. This insect-eater rarely takes supplementary food from bird-feeding areas. Scatter its food under a hedge or in leaf litter. Wrens are in great need of help in hard winters.

BIRD FOOD

The greater the variety of supplementary foodstuffs on offer, the greater the variety of birds that will visit your garden. Use household scraps (avoid anything salty or spicy) or buy from specialist suppliers. Good foods include:

Insectivore mix for robins, blackbirds, thrushes, dunnocks and wrens is vital when the ground is hard. Provide mealworms (available from pet shops and angling shops, or rear your own) or a little tinned pet food.

Fresh coconuts: (never give desiccated coconut): punch two holes (look for the three dark spots at one end – one of them is easy to pierce) and drain out the milk, then saw the nut in half and hang it up for tits.

Peanuts for oils and protein. Use in the shell threaded on string or pushed into bark crevices; shelled in mesh containers; crushed on ground or table for ground-feeders.

Special seedmixtures for wild birds (finches etc.); mixed corn for pigeons, pheasants and ducks; sunflower seeds – very nutritious for many birds, but don't give too much as they are rich in oils.

They will be taken away and stored in crevices by coal tits, marsh tits and nuthatches.

Fats of various kinds are an important source of winter energy for many birds: give pure suet, dripping, meat fat or bacon rinds, in lumps on table or ground, or hanging from branches. Grated dry cheese can also be given. Make 'fat logs' studded with birdseed/nuts. A marrow bone, sawn in half so small birds can reach the marrow is a good source of food. Put out meat bones for corvids, meat scraps for birds of prey and corvids. Stale cakes and biscuits, cooked rice and pasta, cooked potato and uncooked pastry can all be put out.

Windfall apples and pears, halved, are much appreciated by blackbirds, thrushes, tits and robins and are a useful source of moisture in frosty weather too. Raisins and sultanas should be soaked first.

Bread is not the best thing you can provide but it will do if there is nothing else. Crumble and moisten very dry or toasted bread before feeding.

Bird-tables

Bird-tables offer certain advantages to bird feeding:

- they keep food off the ground;
- they can have a roof;
- they can be surrounded with mesh big enough to give access to smaller birds but small enough to keep out the larger greedy species such as magpies, gulls and pigeons;
- they can be kept clean to avoid the likelihood of disease.

It is important that the table should be carefully sited, especially where predators are likely. Most birds feel more secure with an all-round view and with safe cover nearby to which they can quickly escape – say within 3 to 4 metres (10 to 13 feet). But remember that predators also like cover, so avoid low-growing bushes under which a cat could hide. Small bushy trees are usually safer.

There is a huge range of food containers for seeds and nuts. Look for ones that will keep the food dry and that the appropriate birds will find easy to use. (Sometimes they take a little while to get used to a new design, but tits usually learn quickly if the food within is visible.) A simple wire-mesh tube with a solid metal lid and with the base pierced with drainage holes is as good as any for peanuts, unless you have problems with squirrels.

Bird-tables are a lifeline for birds when snow cover makes it difficult to feed on the ground.

SQUIRREL RAIDERS

The major problem for most people who feed birds in the garden is squirrels. There are many different 'squirrel-proof' feeders on the market. These are frequently effective, but squirrels are curious, adroit and determined animals, always looking for ways to beat the system. Pin down some of the foods that squirrels try to take away.

A bird feeder with a strong metal outer cage should give some protection against squirrels.

Occasionally foxes scamper off with half-coconuts though they find it almost impossible to get their muzzles into the shell to eat the flesh. Cats often make off with lumps of fat and will sit coolly on a bird-table eating their way through meat fragments and even dry bread.

Nesting

If you have attracted plenty of winter birds by putting out food, there may be a problem in the spring when there are more birds than there are natural nesting sites. Think well ahead if you want to put up nesting-boxes: they should be in place by Christmas at the latest to give prospective tenants time to get used to them. If you can put them up before the cold weather starts you may well find they are used as winter roosts by small birds such as wrens, who often huddle together in groups for warmth.

Some garden birds are hole-nesters (for example blue and great tits); others

A blue tit nesting-box mimics the tree-hole this bird would normally nest in.

A long-tailed tit by its carefully constructed nest.

prefer nesting platforms of some kind (flycatcher, pied wagtail, blackbird) or open-fronted boxes (robin, wren). Each esting-box should be designed for its intended occupants, and some of their requirements are very specific. For example, the entrance hole has to be just the right size for some species. Several species of owls need a baffle beyond the entrance hole so that they can nest in the dark; and house martins prefer bowl-shaped bases under the eaves of a building.

Nestlings and fledglings

Nestlings too soon out of the nest are in trouble. But first of all be sure that they really are nestlings, not fledglings that are actually ready to leave and are still being fed by their parents.

The main difference between a nestling and a fledgling is feathers! A fledgling cannot necessarily fly, though most are able to do so as soon as they leave the nest. If you find a young bird without feathers it is a nestling. If you know for certain which is its nest, you can try to return it, but be very careful not to disturb its nest-mates.

A feathered young fledgling sitting on the lawn looking lost or hopping about alone is not necessarily in trouble. It is more than likely that a parent is off gathering food, or is in fact out of sight nearby, keeping an eye on it and waiting for you to go away before it brings food to the youngster. Leave it alone: disappear completely to give the parent a chance. Don't return for a couple of hours. If you are worried about predators, gently move the little one under cover close by so that the parents can find it. Do not try to return it to the nest, even if it is unable to fly (owlets often come out of the nest before they can fly), unless you are sure that the nest is empty.

If you are absolutely certain that the parents are not looking after the youngster, think very hard before you commit yourself to adopting it as an orphan. To care for any sick or orphaned wild bird involves considerable time and patience. If you are not prepared to take on this responsibility to the full, don't even start.

Both the male and female bullfinches share the responsibility of rearing their young.

Blue tits

Bullfinch

Goldfinch

Collared doves

Song thrush

Blackbird

Young birds often look a little different from the adults. Here are a few common examples of fledgling birds.

Starling

Robin

Nesting-boxes

Basic nest-boxes require only simple carpentry skills but do make sure the joints are waterproof and include small drainage holes in the floor just in case the water does get in. Use timber thick enough to provide good insulation against heat and cold. Protect entrance holes with metal against intrusive woodpeckers and squirrels and do not treat the wood with preservatives that might put off or, worse, harm the birds!

Site the nesting-box carefully, in a place that is as safe from predators as possible and where there will be minimal disturbance for the birds. Make sure that the prevailing winds will not blow straight into the box (some birds are quite fussy about which way their entrances face) and that it is not always in full sunshine so that the nestlings will not roast inside. Leave the choice and collection of nesting materials to the birds.

Above all, respect the birds' privacy once they have taken up residence and resist the temptation to keep peering in for a look at eggs and young. In particular, keep well away from the nesting-box at laying time and also in the crucial period just before the nestlings are due to fledge: upsetting them at this time could cause a mass premature escape (often called an explosion) when the young birds are not yet fit to be out of the nest.

After the nesting season, clean out your nesting-boxes with soap and water for the sake of good hygiene. Do be aware, however, that some birds are likely to use them as winter roosts so make sure that your housekeeping is done in the autumn.

Only put up owl boxes if the general habitat is suitable: they need to hunt for small mammals and invertebrates, and they need an undisturbed nesting site. Where possible, most owls nest in a dark hole, for example a hollow tree, or on a shaded platform, perhaps in a barn. Tawny owls often nest in lightning-blasted trees. These birds will defend their nests aggressively if disturbed, so take care not to!

The barn owl is a specially protected species. Consult experts from the RSPCA or RSPB if a pair nest in your garden and never disturb a barn owl's nest unless you have a licence to do so. They will quickly desert if bothered.

Little owls nest naturally in hollow trees or branches, finding their way deep into the hollow for safety. The male likes to have a place to perch nearby while the hen is brooding. On no account disturb the birds once they are nesting and do not peer in to look at eggs or chicks. Watch out for premature emergence: the young owlets waddle about on the ground and are easy prey for foxes and cats.

A simple hole-fronted nesting-box for tits.

An open-fronted box placed low down, about a metre (3 feet) above the ground, and concealed by thick, thorny vegetation, will be used by robins and wrens. If placed higher up with a clear approach, flycatchers may use it.

A hollow log can make an excellent nesting-box.

'Nuisance' nests

Buildings, including houses, make ideal roosts and nesting sites for several species of birds, especially those that would naturally use tree-holes, cliff-holes and ledges. They might invade lofts or chimneys, or find a hole in a garden wall, but most head for the eaves, often building behind bargeboards, or in the rafters of open buildings such as barns and garages. Typical building-nesters or wall-hole birds are kestrels, gulls, starlings (who often decorate the nest with flowers), pigeons, owls, swifts, house martins, swallows, pied wagtails, house sparrows, spotted flycatchers, blue tits, great tits, tree creepers and jackdaws.

Sometimes nesting and roosting birds are a source of aggravation to their human hosts. The main problems arise

This swallow has chosen an unusual nesting site – the light still works!

when the nest is in an inconvenient place, bird droppings plaster a patio, nesting material litters the ground below or blocks a chimney, or the parent birds (especially gulls) attack passing humans.

Each problem nest needs to be considered in isolation. You can try blocking up gaps in the eaves during the winter to deter birds the following spring, though starlings, for example, are extraordinarily adept at pulling out weak defences, especially where a traditional roosting and nesting site is concerned. You can fix birdproof cowls on your chimneys. You can offer alternative sites to house martins by putting up your own nest-bowls in a more convenient place – but, like so many birds, they tend to return habitually to old sites. You can install splash-boards to keep droppings off your patio or car. A piece of wood fixed so as to fill in the angle between roof and wall may deter the martins, or lengths of string fixed across the angle of the eaves may prevent them from reaching the corners. However, such action must be taken before the breeding season so as to avoid damaging or destroying the nest of a house martin when it is in use or being built.

Alternatively you could consider yourself lucky to be chosen and learn to tolerate and take a delight in your persistent neighbours.

House martin

Herring gull

Starling

PROBLEMS WITH BIRDS?

There is sometimes a small price to pay for the pleasure of having birds in the garden. Sparrows seem to take pleasure in destroying yellow crocuses and primroses, for example. Bullfinches go for buds on fruit trees and flowering shrubs, but usually only when their preferred seed supplies run out – they like tree seeds, dock seeds, nettle seeds and bramble seeds. Many birds like to share your fruit and vegetable crops, so why not grow enough for all?

Tits occasionally develop destructive habits, famously pecking at silver-top milk bottles to reach the cream. They peck at window putty, too. A tit-pecked bottle of milk can be bad for your health, so keep bottles covered. Recent observations have revealed that magpies and jackdaws have learned the milk bottle trick too.

A blue tit drinks the cream from the top of a milk bottle.

Garden hazards

If you attract plenty of birds, especially to a central point like a bird-table, you inevitably attract their predators as well.

Cats are an obvious hazard for garden birds. Even birds that appear to have been only slightly injured by a cat often die within 48 hours, either from shock or, it is thought, because cats' teeth and claws may harbour bacteria that cause septicaemia in wounded birds. Even if you bell your own cat, you might still have problems with neighbouring cats. Try deterrents such as vigilance and water (cheap) or assorted commercial anti-cat substances and devices (expensive and not always effective). Site bird-feeding areas where cats are at a disadvantage and make nesting-boxes impregnable. There is very little you can do to protect natural nesting sites or inexperienced fledglings from determined cats, however.

Sparrowhawks make lightning raids on garden birds, flashing by so fast that you hardly see them as they scoop up a blackbird or tit in mid-flight. But they make little overall impression on the total population and they are magnificent birds – you are honoured by their presence.

Nest-robbers include, above all, cats and magpies; also jays, crows, jackdaws and rooks, and tawny owls to a lesser extent. Rats, squirrels and sometimes mice also take eggs and nestlings.

SPARROWHAWK OR KESTREL?

Sparrowhawks are fast-flying, agile hunters, weaving at speed between trees or racing along a hedgerow or woodland edge. They have rounded, short wings, giving a few beats and then gliding for quite a distance before flapping briefly again. Their tails are longish and straight.

Kestrels are usually seen hovering on high, maintaining a constant position in the sky, wing tips forward and beating furiously, tail spread, before dropping straight down on to their prey. Kestrels have long, pointed wings and fly steadily.

Nest-boxes might be raided by weasels, great spotted woodpeckers and squirrels. The corvid raids (especially by magpies) distress many bird-lovers but the evidence so far is that these raiders are having little long-term effect on song bird populations.

Foxes might be a problem if you have waterfowl or poultry in the garden. Ensure that waterfowl have an island refuge, especially for nesting, and that it remains inaccessible when the water is frozen. Ensure that poultry are securely shut up at night or have the sense to make for a high roost. Electric fencing can deter foxes.

DISCOURAGING PREDATORS

Just the presence of a dog in the garden will keep many predators away. Chicken-wire can be used to protect bird-tables and nesting-boxes, as long as the mesh is large enough for the birds to get through. It can also be used as a 'funnel' to prevent cats from climbing up supporting poles. Dense hedges, especially evergreens or those that are closely clipped, can be difficult for predators to penetrate and are often chosen by nesting birds.

A weasel will make short work of the contents of a carelessly sited nesting-box.

BIRD CASUALTIES

The handling and treatment of bird casualties is a substantial subject and you would be best advised to seek proper help from those who know how. Wild birds frequently die from shock at being handled by humans. Injured, oiled or sick birds require very careful nursing, feeding and accommodating, and also preparation for their return to the wild in due course. The problem of 'orphans' was considered on page 107.

Swifts are aerial birds. If you find one on the ground, it is in trouble as it will be unable to take off from a flat surface. If there is no obvious injury choose an open grassy site and throw the bird up into the air. This may give it the boost it needs to be able to fly away. If it comes back to the ground, seek assistance.

HAZARDS FROM HUMANS

General hazards such as garden netting and rubbish have been described in Wild Gardens. But there are other hazards that are more specific to birds. People, just by being in the wrong place at the wrong time, can unintentionally keep a parent bird off the nest for so long that the eggs go cold, or cause the parent to scold them loudly and thus draw the attention of potential predators. Worse, people sometimes deliberately look into a nest and distress the birds to the point of desertion or, by moving vegetation, make the nest more visible to predators.

Occasionally birds collide with windows and knock themselves out; or sometimes seeing their reflections will hammer away at the image. Some people use shapes that resemble birds of prey to warn off birds, either stuck to the glass or dangling as mobiles that move in the breeze. If a bird does knock itself out, put it somewhere warm and safe, such as a cardboard box with a few ventilation holes, for an hour or two. If, after a few hours, it shows no sign of recovery, seek specialist assistance from the RSPCA, a local wildlife group or a vet.

Chimneys attract birds such as starlings, jackdaws and owls looking for a roost or a nesting place and, almost invariably, one will fall into the chimney and become stuck – especially the young birds. Make sure that the top of the chimney is birdproofed by using strongly fixed chicken-wire or some form of hood or capping. It's easier than having to dismantle the chimney to remove a distressed bird. Starlings and sparrows also fall into the gap between cavity walls when they nest in the eaves.

Mammals

Strange sounds in the night, musky odours lingering after dawn, patches and holes dug from lawns and flowerbeds under cover of darkness – most people rarely see mammals in their gardens, but there is often other evidence of their presence. Most species of wild mammal are wary of humans and keep well out of sight in daylight hours, but you might be surprised at what goes on in your garden while you are asleep.

Mammal night visitors to your garden, in towns as well as in the countryside, could include foxes, badgers and hedgehogs. Several species of rodent prefer darkness, too, as a time of relatively greater safety from predation. Many gardens are twilight hawking grounds for various species of bat, which often roost and breed under house eaves or in lofts. Rural gardens might be visited by deer at night, and are also likely to be chosen for plant-raids by rabbits at dusk and dawn. Twilight is a good time for mammal-watching, as many are active then. Hunting stoats and weasels might patrol your garden by day and by night.

A foraging band of badgers.

ATTRACTING MAMMALS

Smaller mammals, and a few larger ones, might make their home in your garden, or might simply use it as a meet-and-mate place. For most wild mammals, food is a prime attraction in the garden. Dustbins may attract the larger mammals, but don't automatically blame the wild ones when you find your rubbish strewn all over the place: domestic pets are just as likely to be the culprits. Leaving rubbish out in plastic sacks is simply inviting keen-nosed mammal raiders. Use a secure dustbin.

People often like to encourage garden mammals with food. The problem is that you might not get the mammals you want. If you put out nightly food for, say, a hedgehog, you are also extending an invitation to other mammals, such as rats.

The natural food preferences for different mammals are given in each group's section in the rest of this chapter. It may surprise you to learn that some of them live mainly or entirely on invertebrates. Even badgers prefer earthworms above all. So, once again, in order to attract the bigger animals to your garden, make it a friendly place for the little ones!

GARDEN HAZARDS

Hazards for mammals in the garden include the usual ones described in Wild Gardens – netting, badly designed ponds and pits, thoughtlessly discarded rubbish, poisons and bonfires. Fireworks are another hazard: remember that they can terrify local wildlife just as much as domestic animals.

Foxes

Foxes are highly versatile animals and great opportunists: they have been quick to take advantage of urban as well as rural gardens. They are surprisingly small animals, not very much bigger than miniature poodles under all that thick fur.

FOX HABITS

Foxes tend to eat whatever they can get. In rural areas, foxes prey on voles, mice, rabbits and wild birds; they also eat quite a lot of earthworms, various insects and snails; they take carrion (such as road casualties) very readily and, in season, foxes enjoy berries. In urban areas foxes will have a go at rats and pigeons and help themselves to scraps of every kind, including fruit, vegetables, meat, bones and bird food.

Foxes are usually night visitors, emerging from their daytime cover around dusk (you might catch the green glow of their eyes in torchlight). However, they are often blatantly abroad in the middle of the day and can sometimes be spotted nonchalantly sunbathing in urban gardens. They are opportunists in their choice of living-quarters, tending to shelter in shrubbery and undergrowth, or in convenient dry areas under sheds, without bothering to go underground.

Vixens choose an earth in which to have their litters, often converting an old badger sett or expanding a rabbit burrow. They can be incredibly cheeky when it comes to selecting a good

A red fox shelters under a garden shed.

nursery and might make themselves at home under floorboards and doorsteps, or in attics and cellars. Sometimes they cause damage by chewing at cables and pipes. However, garden sheds are more popular, either underneath or inside: a fox is small enough to squeeze through a gap about four inches square to find a nice, dry place in your shed. A cat-flap is no problem, especially if the smell of food wafts through it.

A recognisable musk is one way of identifying an occupied fox earth; you will also probably see narrow, well-trodden approach paths. Entrance holes are perhaps 25cm (10in) across and taller than those of a badger sett (foxes have longer legs). Foxes are often quite messy and there may be debris such as old bones scattered about nearby.

Foxes will visit your garden if they want to – there's no need to go out of your way to encourage them. Simply ensure that they have peace and quiet, with no dogs to annoy them, and a hide-away to lie up in during the day. If you feed them, put the food out at a regular time just before dusk. They will probably turn up shortly afterwards, determined to take their fill before other animals do so. Most foxes take their food away rather than eating it on the spot, and hide what they don't immediately eat.

Foxes are not aggressive towards humans; rather, they do their best to keep out of your way unless they know

NIGHT NOISES

SCREAMS: these are contact calls, usually made by vixens, but also by dog foxes. You most often hear them in winter and they can sound like somebody being murdered!

BARKS: three or four sharp 'ow ow ows', sometimes ending with a scream. Both sexes make these winter contact calls. The vixen also has warning sounds for her cubs, ranging from a quiet cough to a very loud bark. The cubs themselves give three or four little yelps to make contact.

you well. The only time they might be dangerous is if cornered, when naturally they will try to protect themselves. Foxes are not dangerous carriers of disease either, though there is a possibility that a mangy or wormy fox might infect dogs. The only real problem would be an outbreak of rabies, which could be transmitted by foxes to cats and dogs.

ORPHAN CUBS

All too often, people find what they assume to be an orphaned fox cub and try to adopt it. In most cases the cub has not been abandoned at all and the would-be rescuers should have left it well alone. Bear the following facts in mind if you find a young fox:

- Young cubs are chocolate-coloured and puppy faced. By the age of about six weeks they have more of the red colour of the adult and their faces look more like their parents.
- A vixen doesn't live with the litter after the age of about two weeks. She simply returns at intervals to feed them. Other adult foxes will also feed the litter, especially if the vixen dies. They will do a much better job of it than humans.
- A vixen sometimes moves her litter to other quarters although not necessarily all at once. She may come back for the rest the following night. As the weather warms up, a vixen will probably move her cubs to cooler quarters above ground to lie up under a bramble patch or in an outbuilding. This is when cubs are sometimes seen playing in gardens, apparently by themselves.
- It is most often in April and May that people find what they think is an orphan fox. If you see what appears to be an abandoned cub or litter, do not jump to conclusions. Leave them alone and keep a discreet eye on them. The chances are that the vixen will return for her young.
- If a small cub is in serious danger from predators in daylight, put it safely in a box bedded with clean straw, with minimal handling, and take it back to the earth (or to wherever you found it) around dusk so that the vixen can find it easily. Contact the RSPCA for advice and for an excellent booklet on handling orphan foxes.
- If cubs that are playing or sunbathing in your garden look contented, they are more than likely being cared for by their own mother or adult relatives.
- If they look hungry and dejected and tend to hang around the entrance of their earth making plaintive calls or wander about aimlessly, and there are no fresh remnants of food, then it is possible that they are indeed neglected orphans. But even then the best answer is not to capture them. Instead, leave appropriate food outside the earth on a regular basis. Offer meat bones, road-accident bird and mammal carcasses, bread soaked in fat and household scraps (avoid too much tinned petfood). Do not let them become familiar with humans.

A sleeping red fox.

Fox signs

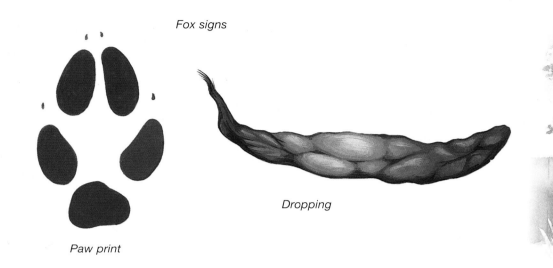

Paw print

Dropping

Earth entrance

PROBLEMS WITH FOXES

There are a few disadvantages to having foxes in your garden:

- you will need a tip-proof, rip-proof, firmly-lidded rubbish bin;
- you might be alarmed in the middle of the night by their screams and other calls, or by the fact that they set local dogs barking;
- if you have chickens or pet rabbits and guinea-pigs, you will have to take extra steps to protect them from harassment and predation;
- you might find holes dug in lawns and flowerbeds.

Most people, especially in urban areas, have a strong admiration for foxes and like having them around even when they are a bit of a nuisance. Anyway, are you quite sure that it is a fox that is causing the problem?

DETERRING FOXES

There is very little point in killing a fox that comes into your garden: as long as the garden remains an attractive source of food and shelter another one will take its place. Your first step, if you are really unable to tolerate the presence of a fox, is to make the garden less attractive:

- ensure that birdfood is inaccessible (foxes are good jumpers but not very good climbers so have a high table);
- ensure that rubbish is inaccessible;
- use electric fencing to protect soft fruit and poultry;
- use an approved animal repellent to deter foxes from making an earth under your shed. Do not use creosote: it will harm the feet not only of foxes but also of cats and dogs. Never try to fill in an earth without checking that it is unoccupied, especially by cubs.

Foxes will raid any food sources they can reach, including low bird-tables.

Badgers

Badgers are mustelids, a family that is on the whole carnivorous, but they will eat just about anything they find.

You are much more likely to smell or hear badgers than to see them. They can emit a potent musk, especially if frightened, and they mark their territories and regular routes with a musky yellow oily liquid. Their footprints are instantly identifiable: a sausage-shaped pad with the round toe-prints aligned along the front. They are very powerful animals, especially at the front end, and can dig or push or bash their way through almost anything. Their jaws are to be feared – a badger has a vice-like bite that is almost impossible to shake off and it will also rake you with its strong, long claws. Never handle a badger unless you know what you are doing.

Badgers dig their setts in a wide variety of locations, including under garden sheds, and a good sett will be used for many generations. They are nocturnal animals, spending the day underground. Their living quarters are lined with bedding (grass, bracken, leaves, straw), which the badgers often 'air' outside the sett and regularly replace with fresh material gathered during the night.

The adults have a range of strange night sounds: a staccato bark, a 'creak' like a moorhen, a deep growl or a throaty purr that rises to a climax during mating, all sorts of snorting and snuffling and grunting and lip-smacking and whickering, and sometimes some fairly alarming screaming.

A badger emerges from a hedgerow.

Fore foot   *Hind foot*

FOOD FOR BADGERS

Badgers have hugely varied diets and will eat almost anything given the chance, including small rabbits, rodents, shrews, moles and even hedgehogs (leaving the spiny pelt turned inside out); frogs and toads; slugs and snails; wasps (including grubs and adults from the nest), bumble-bees, beetles, cockchafer grubs, daddy-long-legs and their grubs (leatherjackets) which they dig out of turf, and carrion. They also enjoy root vegetables and all kinds of fruit, nuts, grass, clover and grain. But above all, the badger's staple diet is earthworms, which it will eat by the hundred.

Garden badgers are fond of peanuts (but not salted peanuts) and they also appreciate tinned pet food. Other suitable foods to offer them include lightly-boiled meat, cheese, chopped apples, carrots, cooked potatoes, acorns, blackberries, windfall orchard fruit and road-killed birds and mammals. Don't put out anything sweet enough to rot their teeth. Ensure that they have a supply of drinking water by fixing a stable container such as a poultry trough or a firmly secured upturned dustbin lid.

It is particularly important that you continue to feed your badgers as they fatten for winter (although they do not actually hibernate badgers reduce their activity in the winter and live mainly off the fat which they have stored in the autumn months) and when the females are suckling in spring and early summer.

In the garden a badger might well dig up your lawns and beds looking for worms and grubs, especially if conditions elsewhere are too frosty or dry for digging. In such seasons, make a point of keeping an area of the garden watered so that badgers can root around. This can save the life of young badgers in particular in times of summer drought. You could also put out food and water for them when it is really dry.

It is a delight and an honour when badgers accept you as their host and you can quietly watch them feeding in the garden after dusk. You must forgive their table manners if they decide to search for their natural food as well, to give your dustbin a roll, to exercise their claws on tree trunks, or to raid your fruit or swipe your corn-cobs (try electrified sheep-netting as a deterrent). Sometimes they will dig latrines in flowerbeds and lawns in spring. But they do a lot of good for gardeners by eating pests.

If you really cannot tolerate badgers, ensure that there is as little as possible to attract them to the garden in the first place – including ensuring that there is no bird-food at badger level.

Badgers continue to use established routes even when humans build motorways across them or put up

PROBLEMS WITH BADGERS

housing estates. If badgers make a nuisance of themselves by knocking down or digging under your garden fence, the animals were probably there first. The best idea is to install a 'badger gate' giving them access to their old route. You must locate it precisely at the point they have always used, however, or the badgers will still find their own way through.

BADGERS IN TROUBLE

Sometimes a sick or injured badger will take refuge in a garden or a shed. Do not take matters into your own hands: contact the RSPCA or a local veterinary surgeon for help. The same applies in the case of orphan cubs: please do not try to adopt them yourself. You should also be aware that badgers now have considerable protection under the law: it is an offence to possess or control a live badger, except under licence.

Fitting a gate on a regularly travelled badger route can help to prevent expensive problems arising.

Hedgehogs

Hedgehogs are frequent night-time visitors, although many people are unaware of their presence in the garden at all. You might see one at twilight, but if you see one in broad daylight it is probably in trouble. If you slip quietly into the garden after dusk, you might catch sight of a hedgehog or two by torchlight, or you might hear them snuffling about for food.

A HEDGEHOG HAVEN

Gardens can be a great boon to hedgehogs – that is, if they can reach them safely without being flattened by traffic on the way and can avoid being massacred by garden strimmers when they are snoozing in patches of rough grass and weeds. They are wanderers, and your garden is likely to be only one of several that an individual animal will visit each night. You are also likely to be visited by several different animals at different times.

Hedgehogs like damp, grassy places in the garden; they like bits of garden wilderness with leaf litter and bramble patches; they like an old log-pile or compost heap or other undisturbed heap where they can find invertebrate food and can spend the winter safely; they like the overgrown area at the base of a hedge, and they like rooting about in shrubberies. Sometimes they nest under thick ivy against a wall or fence, or take a nap hidden by honeysuckle and other climbers.

You can make artificial shelters for hedgehogs. These can be as simple as a board leaning against a pile of bricks, or an upturned crate covered with stones and bricks (you could turn it into a rockery by planting it appropriately). Or, if you are handy, you could fashion a smart nest or hibernation box, though there is no guarantee it will be used by a hedgehog.

HEDGEHOG HAZARDS

Hedgehogs seem to be accident-prone and are the main victims of the hazards outlined in Wild Gardens – netting, ponds, pits, rubbish, bonfires, chemicals and strimmers all pose problems for the unwary hedgehog.

They are ardent investigators and are adept at getting themselves into things,

A hedgehog forages in a garden.

FLEAS AND THINGS

Hedgehogs often harbour a lot of fleas, but these won't be transferred to you or to your pets and they usually don't seem to worry the hedgehog either. Do not use pet flea sprays on a hedgehog, even if the flea burden seems excessive. Ask your pet shop for a powder suitable for birds, which will be much safer for the hedgehog.

Ticks and mites might also cause problems. Individual ticks need to be removed without leaving their mouthparts embedded in the hedgehog. Mites are usually microscopically small and difficult to detect but their effects can be noticeable, including mange, eye infestations, ear inflammation and fits. The best thing to do is to seek veterinary help.

As hedgehogs eat invertebrates, they also eat whatever you might be using to kill your slug and insect pests; they will actually eat slug pellets, especially when they have been softened in the rain. So find other ways of protecting your plants from slugs. If you insist on using pellets, make them inaccessible to hedgehogs by placing them in pipes or under slates, and also remove killed slugs before the hedgehogs eat them.

but hopeless at getting themselves out again. Also, like toads, their reaction to a threat is to keep still: they simply curl up into a ball, which is no defence against machinery or fire. Always make sure that there are no hedgehogs hiding in your bonfire before you set light to it.

FOOD FOR HEDGEHOGS

Hedgehogs eat mainly beetles, caterpillars and earthworms and also slugs, snails, flies, centipedes, spiders, lizards, mice, birds' eggs and carrion. If you want to feed garden hedgehogs, please do not offer only bread and milk: too much of it is more likely to give them diarrhoea than to sustain them. Fresh water is better for them than milk, and they are thirsty animals. They like tinned pet food, but give it in moderation and don't give fish-based food. Put it out just before you go to bed at night.

If the feeding dish has been turned upside down, that is pretty good evidence of a visit by a hedgehog – it may or may not have eaten the food before a cat did, but it will then have had a look underneath for juicy invertebrates.

Crucial times when supplementary feeding will truly be welcomed by hedgehogs are when the ground is hard from drought; when the animals are fattening themselves for the coming winter and when the sows are lactating.

HIBERNATION

Most hedgehogs begin to look for a spot to hibernate around October, depending on the weather, and usually they remain tucked away until March or even April. This is a crucial time in the life of any hedgehog and it is essential for them to have accumulated sufficient weight to see themselves through hibernation.

Hibernation nests might be built under a shed, under a heap of brushwood, leaves, logs, grass-cuttings or bonfire material, or in the cover of a bramble bush. Occasionally a hedgehog might choose to go down a burrow of some kind. The nest, a chamber at the end of a short tunnel, is thickly lined with packed leaves. Those leaves are essential to a successful hibernation nest: if you want to help a winter hedgehog, make sure there are plenty of deciduous leaves about the place.

YOUNG HEDGEHOGS

Most hedgehog sows give birth in June and July, in carefully built nursery nests. Please do not search for a nest: the mother is likely to eat her young if the nest is disturbed soon after the birth. Later, she is more likely just to move the white-spined little ones to a safer place.

The young hedgehogs begin to leave the nest at about three weeks old and are weaned between four and six weeks. Soon after this they disperse to become more or less solitary animals, fending for themselves.

Sometimes there are later batches of young born after mid-September. This means that they do not have time to accumulate sufficient fat for hibernation. Young hedgehogs need to reach a weight of at least 450g (1lb) if they are to have any hope of surviving the winter.

If you come across an underweight young hedgehog in autumn, it needs help. Bring it indoors and keep it somewhere in which the temperature does not fall below about 10°C (50°F).

Feed it until it is big enough to build its own hibernation nest. Give it a varied diet including, say, fresh liver, minced meat, tinned dog food, scrambled egg, etc., mixed with crushed dog biscuits or bread. Always have fresh drinking-water available. When the hedgehog weighs at least 450g (and preferably up to 650g) you can release it at night when the weather is mild and dry, near a potential nesting site with materials to hand. Lean a piece of hardboard against your garden shed, with a supply of dry leaves or old newspaper; or, for preference, release the animal into an area of shrubbery or woodland. Of course the hedgehog may or may not accept your choice of hibernation site.

If you are prepared to keep feeding it all winter in a safe place the hedgehog does not need to hibernate. But do not humanise it, and do be aware that such a youngster will have an awful lot to learn about real life in the wild when you release it in the spring.

In contrast to orphan foxes, hedgehogs that are overwintered in captivity usually do very well after their return to the wild as long as certain rules are followed:

- you must keep the animal as wild as possible and avoid handling it as much as you can. If the hedgehog becomes unnaturally tame it may fail to roll up the next time it encounters a predator;
- if a captive hedgehog becomes active before late March, and if it then weighs over 700g (over 1½lbs), feed it only minimally. You want to encourage it to resume its hibernation. and to avoid it becoming over-weight;
- do not release the hedgehog back into the wild until there is clear evidence that the local hedgehogs are active again, and that a regular natural nocturnal food source (worms, slugs, beetles) is available.

The front footprint of the hedgehog is overlaid by the back foot, forming a single large print.

Moles

You are far more likely to see a molehill than a mole as these animals very rarely put in an appearance above ground.

Moles don't like soils that are very acid, shallow, stony or waterlogged. Their favoured habitats are permanent pasture and woodland, environments that can be similar to those offered by some gardens, where the digging is easy and the food is abundant. A mole's diet consists mainly of earthworms, but it will also eat beetle larvae, fly grubs, slugs and snails and the occasional frog. They often store up a heap of earthworms for winter eating.

Moles have very regular habits and you can almost set your clock by their activities: they are active for a non-stop three to four hours and then rest for three to four hours, repeating the cycle day and night.

Moles are aggressive loners, though you might find it hard to believe that just one mole is probably responsible for all the heaps and tunnels in your garden. Those tunnels can serve a useful purpose in helping to drain your land, though from the mole's point of view the tunnels mainly act as food-traps and as living quarters that are safe from predators. The molehills are simply spoil-heaps of dug-out soil from the deeper tunnels, which the mole pushes upwards through a vertical shaft.

The mole's tunnels range in depth from outer feeding runs just below the surface (which can be a nuisance when your wheelbarrow sinks into them) to permanent deep runs that are perhaps 70cm (27in) down.

If you really cannot tolerate moles in your garden then you have a difficult problem to solve. Many methods have been used to try to deter moles from an area but to little avail. There have been some interesting experiments with chemical repellents recently that may bear fruit in the future.

Traps can be set to kill moles but their successful setting is something of an art and they do not always kill the mole instantly. Poison gases and strychnine can still be used legally against moles but these substances are highly dangerous and must be handled carefully. The best course of action in dealing with problem moles in the garden would be to seek professional help and advice from a reputable pest control agency.

However, it is quite possible to live with moles, once they have established their main networks. Carefully take away the fresh heaps of soil if they are a problem and use it for planting. The mole might heave up a little more once or twice but thereafter the system is usually settled and there won't be any more heaps until next season. If a new heap appears in frosty weather, water it in the evening. By morning it will be frozen and you can simply lift it away with a spade.

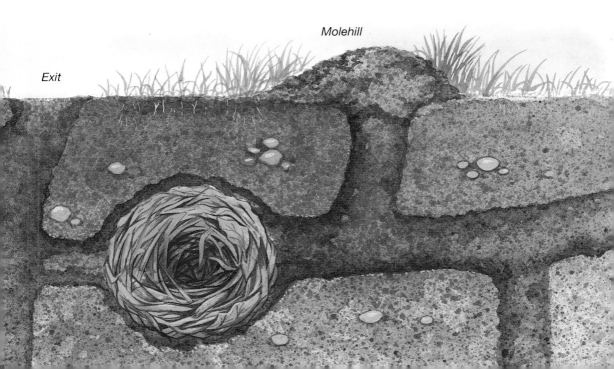

Molehill

Exit

Bats

Bats are incredibly interesting animals and it is well worth overcoming any prejudices you might have about them. Bats do not get tangled in your hair. They might swoop low over your head if you are in their feeding area, but their sonar is far too sensitive for close contact. There are no European vampire bats. All our bats eat nothing but insects; they certainly do not drink blood! Bats do not carry disease – you are not at risk from them in any way.

Bat droppings are harmless. They are dry, in contrast to the sliminess of fresh mouse droppings or the rock-hardness of old ones, and simply crumble to a powder.

Bats don't actually want to come into your bedroom or living room. If they do, their main aim is to get out again. If you are worried, use net curtains over open windows in summer.

Bats are not rodents – they do not gnaw. They won't damage your loft or your electrical wiring or anything else. You might be able to detect a very slight 'batty' smell near a bat roost but it is not unpleasant. They don't like dirty roosts.

Bats do not make nests, nor do they lay eggs! They give birth to live young, like any other mammal, and they do so while hanging from a nursery roost.

Bat noises are really very minor. They patter about a bit (but more quietly than mice); they chatter to each other a bit, but the sound is usually so high-pitched that you have to listen for it; and the babies might squeak a little when mum isn't there, but nothing more than that. They make very good neighbours.

Bats are strongly protected by the law. You may not kill, injure or disturb roosting bats; nor may you damage or block access to their roosts; and you must have a licence if you wish to handle a bat (except if you are taking care of an injured animal). Bat groups are excellent sources of help and advice on all aspects of bats.

When you see a bat at close quarters, you will appreciate why bat-lovers become so passionate about their subject. Children in particular are quickly won over by these very tiny, fragile-looking creatures with their soft fur and bright little eyes.

The face of a pipistrelle bat.

ATTRACTING BATS

Bats need a good larder of insects, a quiet place to roost during the day, a nursery roost for mothers to rear their single young, and an undisturbed winter roost for hibernation. So, if you want to attract bats, provide them with good roost sites (this is very important, natural sites are fast disappearing) and make sure there is a plentiful supply of night-flying insects in your garden by growing night-scented plants. Have a garden light turned on at dusk to attract the insects, and hence the bats; have a pond, which will be a breeding place for the many insects that spend the early part of their lifecycles in water; leave piles of rotting logs undisturbed as invertebrate habitats.

Most bats eat midges, mosquitoes, gnats, various flies (especially caddisflies, craneflies and mayflies), moths and beetles. The main burst of insect activity at night is about two hours after sunset and just before dawn; hence most bats emerge shortly after sunset. But insects are deterred from flying by rain, wind and bright moonlight, and often bats will not bother to emerge in such conditions.

HOUSE ROOSTS

Prospecting bats will look for somewhere quiet, draught free and fairly clean, with a means of access, which need be no more than a tiny slit or hole. Most species prefer a high roost, such as the gable end of a house, but some will take up residence in open porches, under window eaves or even in cellars if there is access for them. Consult your local bat group about simple ways of making your house a more attractive roosting site for your bats.

BAT ROOSTING BOXES

These can be fashioned much in the style of bird-boxes except that the entrance is a narrow slot underneath the box. Use untreated, rough-surfaced sawn timber at least 2cm (3/4in) thick or a hollowed log. The most successful boxes are placed where alternative roosts are scarce, and in a position that feels the warmth of the sun for part of the day, high up on a tree trunk (or house) and with an unobstructed approach for the bats.

WHICH BAT?

There are some 900 known bat species world-wide but only 14 are resident in Britain. Far more species are found in southern England than in the north of Scotland.

Greater horseshoe bat

Serotine bat

Brandt's bat

Barbastelle

Bechstein's bat

Whiskered bat

Leisler's bat

Natterer's bat

A brown long-eared bat circles a tree as it hunts insects.

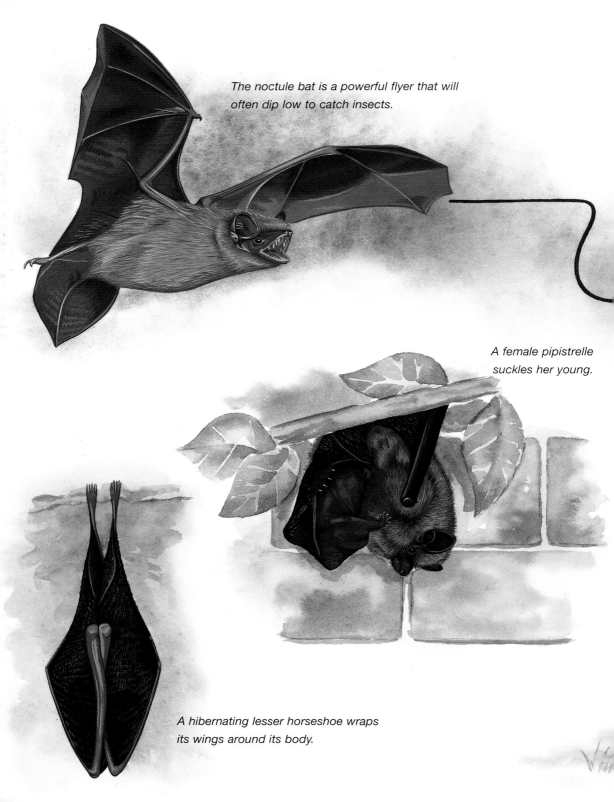

The noctule bat is a powerful flyer that will often dip low to catch insects.

A female pipistrelle suckles her young.

A hibernating lesser horseshoe wraps its wings around its body.

The long-eared bat can fly deftly through tree branches in its search for prey.

The pipistrelle is a fast flyer that twists and dives as it pursues insects.

BATS IN TROUBLE

If a bat enters the living area of your house (as opposed to its roost in the loft) leave a window or door open so that it can escape of its own accord.

Sometimes bats enter a room in the autumn, possibly looking for a winter roost. More often the house bat is a youngster who has made a mistake, and you will probably find it sound asleep in a fold of the curtains in the morning. If the bat is hanging somewhere (rather than in flight), leave it alone and at dusk gently cover it with a soft cloth and carefully pick it up without squeezing. It is unlikely to bite, but wear gloves if the thought worries you. It might squeak a little, especially if it is a youngster. Release it outside – gently! Don't fling it into the air in the hope that it will fly. Ideally, let it hang on a rough vertical surface outside or perhaps amid ivy on a tree. Bats need to warm up properly (by shivering) before they can fly.

Baby bats are sometimes found on garden paths under their roost in the heat of a summer's day. Any bat on the ground in daylight is stranded. A juvenile particularly is in trouble. Pick it up and move it so that it is not vulnerable to predators. A very young bat should be placed as close as possible to the roost entrance so that its mother can take charge. If you do not know where the roost is, put the bat in a ventilated box and then take it outside at dusk.

The main dangers to bats are from cats and pesticides. Some cats make a habit of waiting near a roost exit and swiping at the bats as they emerge. Owls, raptors and mustelids occasionally prey on bats but the animals are more likely to die from starvation than predation. If you find an injured or sick bat, get expert help at once via the RSPCA or your local bat group.

A tiny pipistrelle is small enough to sit on an adult human's thumb. These are the most common of the British bats and the most likely to be found roosting in buildings.

Shrews and rodents

Shrews are not rodents, like mice, but insectivores, like moles. They look very different from mice, with a long snout that is narrow and tapered. The land species are highly active at any time of day or night, but especially around ten in the morning and ten at night. Shrews hunt mainly earthworms and beetles but also take other invertebrates. They need to eat at least three-quarters of their own body weight every day, and even an hour without food is too long for a shrew.

Voles are quite easy to differentiate from mice: they have a rounder look, with blunt noses, small ears, small eyes, shorter tail and legs and a longer, shaggier coat. Bank and field voles are both found in gardens and look rather similar, except that the bank vole is a richer, reddish brown colour. It is active both day and night and is mainly vegetarian but will also eat insects, worms and moth cocoons. Field (or short-tailed) voles eat grass. Both species are an important diet item for a wide range of predators such as owls and raptors, mustelids and foxes.

The common shrew is a very active animal.

Bank vole.

House mouse

Common dormouse.

Water vole

Wood mouse.

Fat dormouse

Field vole

Brown rat

Water voles, sometimes mistakenly called water rats, have a typically blunt and rather chubby vole face and a hairy tail that is shorter than a rat's. Their short little ears only just protrude above the shaggy brown coat. They are shy animals and live on well-vegetated banks by rivers, ponds and drainage ditches.

MICE AND RATS

Mice and rats have longer tails than voles with rather pointed muzzles, large eyes, large rounded ears, sleek rather than rough coats, and longer hindlegs. The wood mouse (also known as the long-tailed field mouse) and the yellow-necked mouse are mainly nocturnal and most active at dawn and dusk. Both

have bigger eyes and ears than house mice, and they don't have that characteristic house mouse smell. Both are found in gardens, where they eat seedlings, buds, fruit, nuts, snails, caterpillars and centipedes, and also fungi, moss, bark and earthworms. The stronger, bolder yellow-necked is the better climber and more likely to come into your loft (a wood mouse prefers outhouses) and its gnawing capacity is amazing. Both species sometimes make their nests in bird-boxes.

Never pick up either of these mice by the tail: they will shed the skin and eventually lose that part of the tail. Yellow-necked mice are more likely to bite if you handle them.

A young brown rat explores a potting shed.

A harvest mouse.

Harvest mice are pretty and dainty little animals that look more like voles than mice. The long tail has a prehensile tip and is used to help them clamber among the stalks. You might be lucky enough to have them in rough areas of a country garden. They eat insects, seeds and berries.

House mice are easily recognised by most people and are most readily identified by their habits and their smell. They can squeeze through the tiniest holes and are superb climbers, jumpers and swimmers, great exploiters of the human race and mainly nocturnal. They eat whatever humans eat as well as seeds and insect larvae.

The common rat is much larger than a mouse. It does not usually live in the house but makes burrows (sometimes under outhouses), leaving a tell-tale heap of soil nearby. Its regular runs are usually obvious. Rats prefer grain but will eat almost anything. They frequent urban areas and farms and may form colonies in rubbish tips and sewers. Like house mice, rats can carry disease. They are nocturnal. You might catch the dull red glow of a rat's eyes in torchlight.

DORMICE

The very small, bushy-tailed common dormouse strips off honeysuckle bark to make its nest in shrubbery and dense undergrowth. It eats nuts, fruit and berries and hibernates during the winter. The related fat or edible dormouse is twice the size and could almost be mistaken for a small grey squirrel. A nocturnal animal, it lives at a higher level, in the tree canopy, and sometimes comes into lofts.

A hibernating dormouse.

Squirrels

Europe's indigenous squirrel is the increasingly rare red, which has retreated in the face of competition from the larger, heavier and more aggressive grey squirrel, introduced from the United States. It is usually easy enough to tell the two apart, by their colour and by the red's long winter ear tufts, but some greys have quite a lot of red in the coat.

Squirrels live in tree-top dreys or in tree-hollow dens. Reds tend to favour conifers (pine, spruce, larch) for their dreys and their food, whereas the greys are usually to be found in hardwood forests (especially oak), parks and gardens. Grey squirrels are great opportunists and will nest in rabbit holes, roof thatch, under tiles or in roof insulation, in church towers and cavity walls and in birdboxes.

Both species are daytime animals active from about half an hour before sunrise to half an hour after sunset; they are particularly active for the first three or four hours of the day, and around midday in winter.

BIRD-TABLE BANDITS

Squirrels are persistent and canny raiders of food put out for birds. All sorts of devices have been created to keep squirrels off birdfood but most squirrels soon find their weak spots. One answer is to make a squirrel-proof birdfeeding area, at the same time providing a squirrel table. Set the bird-table well away from squirrel perches and give it a slippery supporting pole with a squirrel-deflecting collar. Site the squirrel-table close to hedges, trees and bushes. Give them a variety of nuts and seeds but make sure that they have only small quantities of oil-rich items like peanuts and sunflower seed. Peanuts in quantity are particularly bad for young, growing animals.

Squirrels don't hibernate! They might tuck themselves into their dreys for a day or two in hard weather but they do not accumulate enough fat to last them for much longer than that. They are normally active at some stage for every day of the year, but in winter they tend to be so only for the first two to three hours after dawn.

If you find a squirrel in trouble, be extremely careful about handling it as it has a most ferocious bite and will be determined to use it. Wear very thick gloves or summon expert help. Squirrels are absolutely crawling with fleas, which don't usually bite humans but might well transfer themselves to your dog.

PROBLEMS WITH SQUIRRELS

The major problems, apart from birdfood raiding, are holes dug in the garden (to bury food or look for it – including bulbs), the potency of sprayed scent when squirrels are in competition, bark-stripping (which can kill trees, especially saplings), and the destructiveness of squirrels who decide that your loft is a good place to be.

Loft invasion can be more than just a noisy nuisance. Squirrels are rodents and will gnaw their way through electrical cables and even pipes. Talk to your local authority's environmental health department about how best to dissuade them. You will need very robust defences to keep squirrels out once they have discovered a loft. Strong wire netting, such as weldmesh or hexagonal 16 gauge mesh of no more than 25mm (1in), fixed firmly over or wedged into any access points is probably the best solution. You could also try repellent smells.

You should be aware that it is illegal to try to shift the problem on to someone else by trapping a squirrel and releasing it elsewhere.

Grey squirrel

Red squirrel

Rabbits and deer

Rabbits can wreak havoc in country gardens. They have the annoying habit of simply cutting off a stem from a flower or plant and then leaving it lying untouched.

Your best defences are a dog that plays outside, or surrounding the garden (or at least vulnerable planted areas) with small-mesh chicken-wire buried just under the surface to prevent digging under and high enough to prevent jumping over (very expensive).

Repellents don't seem to bother most rabbits. You could try planting things that rabbits don't like to eat such as hypericum, day lilies, daffodils, snowdrops, cyclamen, yellow flag, clematis, rhododendrons, box, laurel, prickly things and most berry-producing plants. In the wild rabbits tend to ignore nettles, ragwort, hemlock, brambles, bracken, foxgloves and scarlet pimpernel.

Deer are also mainly rural rather than urban visitors and are usually very shy animals. They have a passion for roses, especially buds that are just about to flower – thorns do not deter them – and they love runner beans.

Deer in the garden can give so much pleasure that it is worth sacrificing your plants. You might try erecting a large fruit cage to protect the vegetables you really want to keep for yourself.

If deer are a severe problem and you can't just sit back and enjoy them, you will have to fence the whole garden to a height of at least 2m (6½ft) or grow a dense, thorny hedge of the same height – if you can protect the young hedging plants from being eaten in the first place! Another possible solution is an electric fence tape (but never electric mesh).

You can tell which animal has been chewing your shrubs and roses: rabbits make a very neat angular cut but deer are less precise and leave a tag behind.

Above: An alert wild rabbit.

Right: A muntjac deer.

Further Reading

Badgers, Michael Clark, Whittet Books, 1988

Bats, Phil Richardson, Whittet Books, 1985

Birds in Your Garden, Nigel Wood, Hamlyn, 1985

Collins Complete Guide to British Wildlife, N. Arlott, R. Fitter, A. Fitter, HarperCollins, 1981

Collins Field Guide: Birds of Britain and Europe, Roger T. Peterson, Guy Mountfort, P. A. D. Hollom, HarperCollins, 5th edition, 1993

Collins Field Guide: Insects of Britain and Northern Europe, Michael Chinery, HarperCollins, 3rd edition, 1993

Collins Field Guide: Mammals of Britain and Europe, David Macdonald and Priscilla Barrett, HarperCollins, 1993

Collins Field Guide: Reptiles and Amphibians of Britain and Europe, E. N. Arnold, J. A. Burton, D. W. Ovenden, HarperCollins, 1978

Hedgehogs, Pat Morris, Whittet Books, 1994

The Living Garden, Michael Chinery, Dorling Kindersley, 1986

The Living Garden, Geoff Hamilton and Jennifer Owen, BBC Books, 1992

Nest Boxes for the Birds of Britain and Europe, Lennart Bolund, Sainsbury Publishing Ltd, 1987

Nestboxes, Chris du Feu, British Trust for Ornithology, 1993

Pond Life, Trevor Beebee, Whittet Books, 1992

RSPB Bird Feeder Handbook, Robert Burton, Dorling Kindersley, 1990

RSPB Book of British Birds, Peter Holden, J. T. R. Sharrock, Pan Macmillan, 1994

Small Wonder, Mari Friend, Blandford, 1991

Snakes and Lizards, Tom Langton, Whittet Books, 1989

Squirrels, Jessica Holm, Whittet Books, 1987

Urban Foxes, Stephen Harris, Whittet Books, 1986

Watching Wildlife: A Field Guide to Wildlife Habitats of Britain, Geoffrey Young, Elaine Parks, George Philip, 1992

The Wild Garden, Violet Stevenson, Frances Lincoln, 1985

Useful Addresses

Royal Society for the Prevention of Cruelty to Animals
Causeway
Horsham
West Sussex
RH12 1HG

Scottish Society for the Prevention of Cruelty to Animals
Braehead Mains
603 Queensferry Road
Edinburgh
EH4 6EA

Bat Conservation Trust
15 Cloisters House
8 Battersea Park Road
London
SW8 4BG

British Trust for Ornithology
The Nunnery
Nunnery Place
Thetford
Norfolk
IP24 2PU

Butterfly Conservation
PO Box 222
Dedham
Colchester
Essex
CO7 6EY

Countryside Council for Wales
Plas Penrhos
Ffordd Penrhos
Bangor
Gwynedd
LL57 2LQ

English Nature
Northminster House
Peterborough
Cambridge
PE1 1UA

Henry Doubleday Research Association
The National Centre for
   Organic Gardening
Ryton-on-Dunsmore
Coventry
CV8 3LG

Herpetofauna Conservation International Ltd
Triton House
Bramfield
Halesworth
Suffolk
IP19 9AE

Mammal Society
15 Cloisters House
8 Battersea Park Road
London
SW8 4BG

Royal Society for Nature Conservation
Wildlife Trusts Partnership
The Green
Witham Park
Waterside South
Lincoln
LN5 7JR

Royal Society for the Protection of Birds
The Lodge
Sandy
Bedfordshire
SG19 2DL

Scottish Natural Heritage
12 Hope Terrace
Edinburgh
EH9 2AS

Scottish Wildlife Trust
Cramond House
Kirk Cramond
16 Cramond Glebe Road
Edinburgh
EH4 6NS

Soil Association
Bristol House
40-56 Victoria Street
Bristol
BS1 6BY

Index